D1553489

Leora's Letters

THE STORY OF LOVE AND LOSS
FOR AN IOWA FAMILY
DURING WORLD WAR II

JOY NEAL KIDNEY

with Robin Grunder

Copyright © 2019 by Joy Neal Kidney

All rights reserved. No part of this book may be duplicated or transmitted by any means without written permission of the author except in the case of brief quotations embodied in critical articles and reviews.

For permission, please write to joynealkidney@gmail.com

Printed in the United States of America

Library of Congress Control Number: 2019916637

ISBN (softcover): 978-1-7341587-0-0
ISBN (ebook): 978-1-7341587-1-7

Available from Amazon.com and other retail outlets

"Meadowlark" Copyright © 2019 Nicholas Dowd

Cover design by Cari Wooten-Fuller & Nelly Murariu
Interior design and layout by Nelly Murariu @PixBeeDesign.com

Cover photo by Emina Hastings

Dedication

To the memories of:

Clabe and Leora Wilson
Delbert Goff Wilson
Donald Woodrow Wilson
Doris Laurayne (Wilson) Neal
Darlene Evelyn (Wilson) Scar
Dale Ross Wilson
Daniel Sheridan Wilson
Claiborne Junior Wilson

For

Kate

and for generations of Americans to come,
to remember just what our freedoms cost

He determines the number of the stars and calls them each by name.

PSALM 147:4

CONTENTS

Van Harden

WHO-Radio Personality

Living in Iowa is indeed a unique pleasure. Sometimes that's hard to describe to someone who has never experienced it. But in this book by Joy Neal Kidney, the Iowa lifestyle and ethic really hit home to me by means of some very, very difficult situations, weathering them and moving forward in spite of them,

The heroine, Leora Wilson, being an Iowa farm wife, losing three sons and being widowed within three short years, and how she carried on after that. And riveting stories of five sons in the military, atomic bombs being dropped, a stroke, broken hearts, and other deep human emotions.

Joy lets us see her grandmother's personal family correspondence through letters. It is heart tugging. Be ready to be moved by this true story.

Meadowlark

Nicholas Dowd

Every morning that summer
Brought a premonition
A sense of something pending
Fencerows buzzed with it
Breezes whispered it to the corn
Meadowlarks sang it at sunrise.
Some nights we wondered
What might lie ahead, but
All we could do was listen
Waiting for the song of the lark
To drift across our fields at dawn.

PROLOGUE

For as far back as I can remember, I spent Memorial Day at the Violet Hill Cemetery in Perry, Iowa. Grandma Wilson called it "Decoration Day," and each year Grandma, Mom, and Aunt Darlene brought along pails of flowers, one from each of their gardens. My sister Gloria and I helped fill the vases with blooms to decorate the four graves there.

On our way back home from the cemetery, we took the route which led past the old acreage south of Perry, where Grandma and Grandpa Wilson had made their home at the end of World War II. The grownups took note each year of how the trees they planted had grown. We also drove by the farmhouse where my grandparents lived and worked before buying their own acreage. This farm at Minburn was the place they lived when I was born.

The ritual was the same every year.

It wasn't until decades later that I learned only two people were buried under the four names on those gravestones.

Grandma Wilson died on her ninety-seventh birthday. After her death, Mom and Aunt Darlene spent weeks reading through old family letters, most of which were written during the war. Many tears were shed as the sisters vividly recalled painful memories their family had endured. My sister and I wondered if it was actually healthy for my mom and aunt to be reliving these stories of war. I asked if I could read the letters.

Once Mom and Aunt Darlene were finished with them, I became the keeper of these documents. There were hundreds of letters, postcards, and telegrams. It was through these letters and saved memorabilia that I began to piece together the World War II story of my grandparents, Clabe and Leora Wilson, and their seven children.

A little background on the Wilson Family:

Clabe Wilson

Clabe Wilson was born in 1888 and grew up in the woods of Guthrie County, Iowa. During the Depression, he enjoyed and depended on hunting and trapping for food, and worked odd jobs to survive. He married Leora Goff Wilson in 1914.

Leora (Goff) Wilson

Leora was born in 1890, the oldest of eleven children. The couple had ten children, including two sets of twins. In 1929 baby twins succumbed to whooping cough. The couple also lost an infant two years later. Their seven remaining children grew up in the small Dallas County town of Dexter. In 1939, the family moved to an 80-acre farm near Minburn, where Clabe and his sons were hired to run all the farming and livestock operations.

Delbert Wilson

Delbert was born in 1915 and joined the Navy a year after graduating from Dexter High School. He felt like he had hit the jackpot as he was getting enough to eat and able to send home $10/month. After Delbert's enlistment was up, he had hoped to find work in southern California, but eventually gave up and returned to Iowa and was farming with his father and brothers.

Donald Wilson

Donald was born in 1916. He graduated in the same class as his older brother, Delbert, and together they enlisted in the Navy. Two years after enlistment, Don took an Electrical Interior Communications course in Washington, D.C. He was later assigned to the crew of the brand-new aircraft carrier USS *Yorktown*.

Doris Wilson

Doris was born in 1918. After graduating from Dexter High School, she was awarded a scholarship to play basketball for the American Institute of Business in Des Moines. The scholarship only covered tuition, so Doris worked at Bishops Cafeteria in return for meals and relied on her Navy brothers to send money home for her room rent. When they couldn't keep up with rent money, she dropped out and worked as a waitress. In 1941, Doris moved a few miles north of Minburn to Perry, where she worked at McDonald Drug, which had a soda fountain and a restaurant section.

Darlene Wilson

Darlene was born in 1921, a twin to Dale. Upon graduation from high school, she hired out to do cooking and housework for families experiencing illness or who had a new baby. In 1941, Darlene married Alvin "Sam" Scar, a farmer from Earlham, Iowa.

Dale Wilson

Dale was Darlene's twin. Without solid plans for the future, he worked hard on the Minburn farm after high school, but had always dreamed of becoming a pilot. He'd even discussed joining the Navy, but his older brothers talked him out of it. It wasn't until the draft began that Dale considered joining the Army Air Force. He took correspondence courses in math so he could eventually become an officer, which pilots were.

Danny Wilson

Daniel Wilson was born in 1923. He attended Washington Township High School where he graduated as valedictorian of his class. Danny looked up to his brothers, and especially admired Delbert, who took physical training seriously. He worked on the Minburn farm after graduation, and was also interested in airplanes.

Junior *Wilson*

Junior was born in 1925. He was known for whistling while he worked. Like Dale and Danny, Junior was enamored with airplanes. When those three brothers were in grade school, they pooled their money and took a ride in an open cockpit airplane. Ever since that experience, all three boys hoped to fly someday.

I am the oldest granddaughter of Clabe and Leora Wilson. *Leora's Letters: The Story of Love and Loss for an Iowa Family During World War II* is my effort to share the story I learned through the hundreds of letters accumulated among the Wilson family. Most chapters include letters, or the essence of letters, written between Leora and other family members, especially her sons in the service. I've imagined how some of the scenes would have played out to weave a narrative thread throughout the story. To stay true to history, as much as possible, I've used the slang they used during this time of war, although some may be considered offensive in this day and age.

The year is 1941. Delbert, Dale, Danny and Junior were all living at home and working on the Minburn farm. Doris lived in nearby Perry, and Darlene and her husband Sam farmed southwest of Earlham.

This story began on the farm with a knock on the door.

CHAPTER 1

Late 1941

Dallas County, Iowa
November 1941

It was after midnight when Leora and Clabe were awakened to the barking of their dog, Spats. Their bedroom was just off the kitchen. *It's probably just a raccoon,* thought Leora. Then she heard a knock, and someone opened the back door.

"Clabe, someone is in the house." She reached for her robe.

"Who is it?" hollered Clabe as he pulled up his overalls over his long johns. They never locked the door, but the neighbors didn't just come in in the middle of the night.

"Don!"

Clabe walked into the kitchen, confused. "Don, who?"

"Dad, it's me, your son." It was then that Clabe recognized his son's voice, and noticed two figures standing just inside the porch.

Leora, wrapped in a robe and deftly lighting an oil lamp with kindling wood aflame from the wood burning stove, joined her husband. "Don, what are you doing home? Did you boys get a furlough after all?"

Don and his buddy shook their heads. "Not exactly. We just got back to the East Coast and it looks like war is about to break out. Who knows if I'd ever get back home again? We hitchhiked to Minburn."

Clabe asked if they were in trouble with the Navy.

"If we aren't now, we will be." By this time all the brothers had clambered down the stairs and Don introduced everyone. "Frank here is in my gang on the Yorktown. Frank, these are my parents and brothers Delbert, Dale, Danny and Junior."

"Pleased to know you all." Frank nodded and shook hands with each. "Don has told me so many stories, I feel like we've already met."

"Well, you boys can sleep down here. We'll talk more in the morning." Leora led Don and Frank to the spare room on the main floor where the Wilson sisters stayed when they were visiting home.

"See you in the morning," Delbert said as he and the three younger brothers headed back up the stairs. "Maybe we can do a little hunting while you're home."

The last to turn in, Leora blew out the lamp, thankful she had set out a big bowl of bread dough to rise the night before. When morning came, all she would need to do was punch it down and divide it into greased bread pans, let it rise, and bake the loaves in a hot oven. She began her night's rest knowing there would be plenty for everyone.

When morning came, Leora stoked the iron stove and started the coffee and had bread already baking. "You boys ready for your cup of joe?" She grinned at Don and Frank who stretched sleepily as they sauntered into the kitchen.

"Sure thing," Don replied. "Something smells great."

"That's the bread. My good hens are still laying, so you can have as many eggs and as much fresh butter as you can eat for breakfast." She'd changed into a cotton housedress with an apron over it.

Clabe and the rest of the boys were out milking and feeding the animals. Junior's signature whistle could be heard as the men headed back towards the house, each bringing in an armload of firewood for the kitchen. They took turns washing up in the enamel wash pan Leora had set out on the porch with warm water from the kitchen stove's reservoir. After the men in overalls had washed up, everyone joined Don and Frank around the sturdy oak table.

"Frank, where are you from?" Delbert asked. "You've got quite a southern drawl."

"Alabam'. My dad's a lawman, so we didn't dare go there! You know we're a part of Roosevelt's Neutrality Patrol, don't you?"

"Well, we knew you couldn't say because of censorship, but that's what we suspected when we learned you were in the Atlantic, and not at Pearl Harbor anymore."

Leora scrambled and served eggs along with a big stack of bread and a crock of butter, as the boys continued to talk. She patted Don on the shoulders and grinned at him.

"Our flattop has been on half a dozen convoys on that big pond." Don grinned back. "This last trip we swapped in the middle of the Atlantic and escorted British ships back here."

Frank shared how nerve wracking it had been with so many German submarines prowling around the Atlantic.

"No wonder you took a chance and came home. Frank, did Donald tell you we joined the Navy together back in '34?" asked Delbert.

"He did, but he said you didn't reenlist."

"No. I hoped I could make more money out of the Navy, but I was wrong. I reckon if war does break out like you suspect, I'll be recalled. Dale here has already had to register for the draft."

Dale, the middle brother, had just turned twenty. The Wilson's landlord kept buying land and livestock, so there was plenty of field-work and chores to keep Clabe and Don's four brothers busy.

"I'd rather join the Air Corps," Dale said. "I'd really like to learn to fly."

"That's what I'd like to do, too," said Danny.

The boys finished eating and the conversation continued as Clabe leaned back and lit his pipe. The scent of tobacco mingling with coffee was a comforting kitchen aroma for the Wilson family.

"What do you Navy boys think about flying?" Delbert asked Don and Frank. "You get to see all that happens to planes and pilots."

"Yah," Donald replied. "I'm sure glad my battle station is several decks down with all the crackups on the flight deck when the fledglings are practicing. You would definitely be safer in the Navy."

Dale grinned. "But the Air Corps planes are better looking."

It was the youngest brother, Junior, who changed the subject. "Who's all going hunting?" Everyone began to back their chairs away from the table and Delbert offered to help find Don and Frank some hunting clothes.

"I'll phone your sisters." Her hair corralled by a hairnet, Leora cleared the table. The Dallas County farmhouse had a phone, but no electricity or running water. "I hope they can both make it over while you're home."

Soon, all five brothers, Frank, Clabe, and the Wilson's beloved terrier-bulldog, Spats, were hiking the hills, guns in hand. As they moved along, the conversation turned to the Wilsons' second hand "smoking Buick."

"Why don't we pool our money while I'm home and get a new car," suggested Donald. "We could at least look at them."

The Wilson sisters, Doris and Darlene, were anxious to see Donald. Doris got the weekend off, and it looked like all seven siblings would be home at the same time, for the first time in years. "Maybe we can get Edmonson's to get a picture of us all." Leora plunged her hands into hot soapy water and began washing the breakfast dishes.

Doris rode the Minneapolis and St. Louis (M & St. L) train to Minburn where one of the boys picked her up. Darlene and husband Sam arrived from their farm near Earlham. What a reunion Donald had with his younger sisters, who were not shy about hugging him. All ten people piled into the old Buick and Sam's car and headed six miles to the nearby town of Perry where they had a family photo taken. While they were there, they indeed traded off their old Buick for a brand-new gray, 1942 Plymouth four-door, 95-horsepower, Special Deluxe sedan with concealed running boards.

Soon, the expected letter from the Navy arrived: *Your son is AWOL. Do you know where he is?* The letter went on with the possible consequences for jumping ship.

After handshakes, pats on the back, and a few snapshots, Donald and Frank turned themselves in to the Navy office in Des Moines. From there they were sent under orders, but not under guard, by train to the Great Lakes Naval Training Station in Illinois. There the Navy kept Donald and Frank busy while deciding what to do with the young sailors.

BACK: Danny, Darlene, Donald, Junior, Delbert, Doris, Dale.
Front: Clabe and Leora Wilson
Last photo of the family, Perry, Iowa, November 1941.

Every day, the Wilsons tuned into the news on their big console radio. There were plenty of reports about the war in Europe. *Perhaps the sooner we get into the scrap, the sooner all of this would be over,* Leora thought to herself.

And then maybe, just maybe, her four other sons wouldn't have to join up after all.

Perry, Iowa
December 7, 1941
Doris

In a gold waitress uniform, Doris Wilson served Sunday dinner to the after-church crowd in the restaurant section of the McDonald's Drug Store. Sammy Kaye's "Sunday Serenade" provided background music over WHO Radio. A news bulletin interrupted the music.

The Japanese had bombed Pearl Harbor.

The calmness at the restaurant was replaced with a flock of questions. "The Japs? Why would they bomb Pearl Harbor?"

"Does this mean we are at war?"

"Where is Pearl Harbor?"

"In Hawaii," Doris answered with a sigh. "And yes, I'm afraid this does mean war. My brothers are all the wrong ages." Doris slumped into a chair as she thought about her brothers being called to duty.

"How many brothers do you have?"

"Five. Don is already in the Navy. His ship was stationed in Pearl Harbor a few months ago. He told us we shouldn't trust the Japs. He was right."

Doris thought about Delbert probably being recalled by the Navy, and Dale having already registered for the draft. She worried about Donald's safety in the Atlantic. Thankful that Danny and Junior were still too young to be drafted, Doris still feared for her family.

❦

Darlene

In her Madison County farmhouse, Darlene also heard the news bulletin about Pearl Harbor. She shouted the news from the window to her husband Sam and his father who were cutting wood in the orchard.

SAM AND DARLENE SCAR, MARCH 1941, DEXTER, IOWA.

❦

Rural Minburn

It was a mild Sunday afternoon out on the Minburn farm when the Wilsons heard the news on their battery-operated radio.

Leora cleaned up from dinner while Clabe and his sons hiked to the field to build a fence. "This country is going to be in a desperate struggle," Delbert said.

"I wonder how soon my number will come up." Dale rolled up his shirt sleeves as he walked. "I want to pass that Air Corps test first."

Delbert warned Dale again that the Navy would be a safer place to fight. "Pilots are out there all alone." And to his dad, "I'm gonna have to go back in, Dad. Danny and Junior will have to help you with work on the farm."

Bulletins continued to interrupt radio programs listened to in the Wilson home. The Japanese had also attacked Singapore, Thailand, Malaya, Guam, Midway, Hong Kong, Wake, and the Philippines.

After morning chores the next day, the Wilsons learned that President Roosevelt was about to address a joint session of Congress. They gathered around the console radio in the living room. Clabe tamped tobacco from a Prince Albert can into the bowl of his pipe and lit it. The embers in it began to glow as he drew air into the pipestem. Danny began to clean one of the guns.

The president announced: *"Yesterday, December 7, 1941, a day which will live in infamy, the United States of America was suddenly and deliberately attacked by naval and air forces of the Empire of Japan. The attack on the Hawaiian Islands has caused severe damage to American Naval and Military Forces. I regret to tell you that many American lives have been lost. In addition, American ships have been torpedoed on the high seas between San Francisco and Honolulu."*

Leora picked up some mending to work on and joined the men around the radio. The aroma of tobacco drifted around the listeners. Roosevelt listed the other places where Japanese forces had attacked. He went on: *"Since the attack by Japan was dastardly and unprovoked, I ask Congress to declare a State of War between the United States and the Japanese Empire."*

The news bulletins named even more places in the Pacific attacked by the Japanese. The Wilsons located the spots in an atlas and discussed where they thought the Japanese would strike next.

"You boys get it all figured out." Leora, a sturdy woman not quite five feet tall, parked her sewing in a wicker basket. "I want to get a letter started to Donald. He'll be looking for one."

"Mom, don't worry." Delbert carried his coffee cup to the sink. "We have a modern navy. I don't think this war will last long."

From a drawer in the buffet, she pulled out writing paper, a bottle of ink, and her favorite pen. "I'll try to get this done in time for one of you to take it up to the mailbox."

Their mailbox was up on the main road, half a mile north.

Five days later, Germany and Italy declared war on the United States. Week after week the radio brought news of Japanese domination in the Pacific, and of dozens of Allied ships sunk in the Atlantic, some right off the East Coast.

Donald and Frank were both ordered back to the *Yorktown*, the ship they had left in Casco Bay, Maine. "Hold your letters until you hear from me," Donald wrote, "for I don't know how long it will be before I catch up with the ship." Donald also said he did not receive a punishment from the Navy for jumping ship. There were far more important things happening in the world for that.

The United States was at war in the Pacific and in Europe. Leora thought of her three brothers who had all fought in the Great War and had come home okay. She drew comfort from this as she thought about her own sons, and prayed they would come through this war. She also prayed that it would all be over before Danny and Junior would have to go.

CHAPTER 2

Early 1942

Dallas County, Iowa
Early 1942

January is the essence of winter in Iowa. There's a stillness and a rhythm of the rat-a-tat of woodpeckers, the rattle of tire chains, the ping of a stream of milk from a cow when it first hits the bucket. Steam rises from the muzzles of cattle and horses. There's frost on the windows, and woodsmoke rising from the chimney from the kitchen stove.

Temperatures would get as low as 36 degrees below zero that winter, and the Wilsons often worked with at least a foot of snow on the ground. Leora wore a housedress, even in winter, but added overshoes, a jacket, and even a headscarf to get some fresh air and make sure her wintered-over chickens were healthy.

Staying busy with farm work kept them from worrying about Donald every minute.

"Surely the United States has built up its Navy and we should be able to beat the Japs, shouldn't we?" asked Junior. He helped with the morning chores and then rode the Washington Township school bus to finish his senior year and play on the basketball team.

"I would certainly think so," said Delbert, ten years older than Junior. "But the Japs are moving so quickly, already winning a battle in the Java Sea and taking Manila in the Philippines."

"They even declared war on the Netherlands," added Danny. "This may turn out to be a more serious war than we think."

The Wilsons received a letter from Donald asking them to address his mail in care of the Postmaster, San Francisco. Delbert explained that this meant Don was heading back to the Pacific and would be in combat before long.

Doris

Doris phoned home for a ride when she arrived at the Minburn Depot toward the end of winter. She rode the M & St. L from Perry on her day off about every other week. Dale picked her up at the depot.

"Thanks for coming for me, Dale. How are the folks doing? Working too hard, I expect."

"Well, Dad's getting ready for baby pigs, hauling feeders and troughs to the south place."

"And I bet Mom is getting ready for her order of baby chicks," Doris added.

"Yes, she and Dad have scrubbed out the brooder house, and even set up a kerosene stove."

It was only a couple of miles before Dale and Doris came to the turn-off north of the Minburn farm. Before turning, Dale stopped at the short row of rural mailboxes and Doris hopped out to check their box.

In it was a letter from Donald.

USS Yorktown
March 6, 1942
Donald

Dear Folks,

Sure did take a long time for Delbert's letter to catch up with me. I think it was around a month ago that I finally received it. I'm in good health, as usual. I'm getting used to a routine of sorts. Don't expect any long letters from me for some time to come. I think if you read the papers you'll get more news of the activity in the Pacific than I could tell you.

Will be looking forward to a letter from you letting me know how Dale made out with that examination. I sure would like to see him make the grade. He'd be a good flyer, I believe.

Delbert may not be called as soon as he expected, since he's running a farm. Gotta have beef to make stew for the sailors to fight now. Well anyway, I hope to hear how everything is going in your next letter. When I'll receive it is an entirely different question.

Time seems to pass rather fast for me. I'm pretty well occupied most of the time which helps. We get the news of what's going on elsewhere via our own press news on board. Sometimes it's a few days old but it's still news to us.

I think I told you about our phonograph that we all chipped in and bought. That breaks the spell and helps relieve the pressure we all have. Let me tell you, that phonograph really gets a workout at times. We've around a hundred records—just about anything you'd want to hear.

The last few years sure have convinced me more than ever that life sure is a big gamble. I hope my number doesn't turn up like everyone else thinks, but sure as shit don't worry any about it. If I see the end of the war, I figure I'll have good tales of experience and travel under the worst condition a man can be in. I'll get me a fishing pole, a broken-down auto, a soap box, and a pocket knife, and let the rest of the world go by.

I can't think of a thing more I could write. Will be looking forward to hearing from all of you soon, I hope.

As always, love,

Donald

"That sure sounds like Don, doesn't it?" asked Dale.

"Yes. But I sure wish he could tell us what is going on," added Leora.

USS Yorktown
April 1942
Donald

Dear Folks,

I got all of your letters at once! It sure was a treat to hear from civilization. You'll have to imagine the excitement from all of us when the mail finally comes aboard after quite a while. It reminds me of Christmas when I was younger.

I also got a letter from a gal I met in Boston.

I'd like to tell you what I'm doing, but it would be blocked out of my letters. Remember what I've said before; when you listen to the news broadcasts and read the paper, only believe a certain percentage of that. Another guy aboard got a clipping from some newspaper giving some propaganda that our ship was damaged or sunk. That's a lot of hooey.

How is Dale doing with his exams? If he makes it, I know he's sure to be one guy in the Air Corps that will give 'em hell.

I heard about the sugar rationing and that the W.C.T.U. (Women's Christian Temperance Union) seem to think they can save a lot of sugar by stopping the production of beer. Those ol' hens are probably backed by some big bootlegger and they don't know it! I sure could go for a couple-a ice-cold Budweiser's right now! Beer is one thing a man looks forward to!

Send pictures if you can. Do you have that one of the whole family before everyone left for the Army? What about the one with me and Frank? Send an extra copy of that so I can share one with him.

Donald

Bleak news reached the Dallas County farm about the surrender of American troops on Bataan, and of more Japanese attacks and invasions. Finally, after weeks of discouragement, news came of the Doolittle Raid and bombing of Tokyo. This was the first time Japanese homeland had been struck.

USS Yorktown
May 1942
Donald

Dear Folks,

Suppose you got the report of the Jap mainland getting its first taste of war. I have to admit that I'm ready for about six months on the farm. I sure do have a better appreciation for the simple life.

You know that watch of mine that is put away? I don't use it or need it. You can make Junior a graduation present of it. It'll give him that distinguished look, you know!
Donald

Junior's senior year was winding down. He was a good student, but when he learned a year ago that Danny had to give a speech at commencement, he made sure he wasn't at the top of his class.

"Guess where our Senior Banquet is going to be," Junior said to his mother.

"In Des Moines," she guessed.

"No. To conserve gas for the war, it's going to be in the banquet room at Doris's restaurant in Perry."

"Will you wear your suit?" Leora asked.

"Nope. Not going."

"Why wouldn't you go to your Senior Banquet?"

"Jack Jackman isn't going. He was on our basketball team but doesn't have money for the banquet or even decent clothes. I think I'll just spend the evening with him. I don't want to dress up in a suit anyway."

The day of the banquet, Jack and Junior did show up at McDonalds. Doris was working the soda fountain and the two boys perched on a couple of stools. "Make us the best chocolate malt you can," ordered Junior. "We're celebrating!"

Doris did just that and paid for them as well.

The meadowlarks had been back for weeks now. Iowa's plum thickets bloomed white against spring's green. Potatoes, onions and lettuce were planted. And the youngest Wilson brother, Claiborne Junior Wilson, graduated from Washington Township High School— the last in the family to finish high school and the first one to wear a graduation robe.

JUNIOR, 1942 GRADUATE OF WASHINGTON
TOWNSHIP SCHOOL

The Wilson's radio brought news reports about a big battle in the Coral Sea. The Japanese reported their victory and the sinking of two carriers. U.S. reports said that a dozen Japanese ships had been sunk, but that no American battleships had been lost.

When the family didn't hear from Donald, they worried that he had been in the battle.

Dallas County, Iowa
May 1942
Delbert

The War Production Board had asked women to save old hose to be made into parachutes and other war necessities. Dale's draft number came up in March, so he took his tests, enlisted in the Air Corps, and waited to be called up.

Doris, wanting to do her part, checked into joining the newly created Women's Army Auxiliary Corps (WAAC).

Delbert rejoined the Navy. Early on the Saturday before Mother's Day, Darlene and Sam pulled into the Dallas County farm to see him off.

"'Bout ready to go?" Darlene walked in from the back porch. "You know, we're pulling for you."

"I'm ready." He stood to shake Sam's hand. "We'll get the Nazis and Japs whipped and be back before you know it." Delbert hadn't helped with the farm chores that morning and was anxious to get going.

"Be sure to write often." Leora gathered the breakfast dishes. "Letters from you boys help us not to worry so much. Write just to tell us that you are all right."

"Well, I'll need your letters to help get me through, too. Even you, Sam."

"Darlene might have to do the writing for the both of us while I'm in the field," Sam answered. "Good luck, Del. We're pulling for you."

Rain threatened but Leora wanted to get one last photo taken before Del left. They went outside for some family snapshots—Delbert in a dark suit and open collared shirt, Darlene and her mother both in cotton house dresses, Leora's covered with her signature apron. Clabe and the youngest brothers, Dale, Danny, and Junior were all dressed in overalls and zippered jackets. Doris couldn't be there as she had to work.

"I'll be sure to write Doris a letter," Del said. "I'm sure she'll write me back right away."

Pipe in hand, Clabe shook hands with his oldest son. "Keep your chin up, son. And be sure to write."

Leora patted his arm and shoulder. "We sure will miss you, Del. Come home as soon as you can."

"I will, but I better get going. Don't you folks work too hard and let me know if you find a small place to buy. You're sure going to need it if Uncle Sam takes all of us boys." And with that, Del slipped into the driver's seat of the family's Plymouth and headed for the depot. Dale and Danny rode along.

Everyone waved as they left the driveway.

CLABE, LEORA, JUNIOR, DELBERT, DALE, DANNY, DARLENE.
MINBURN, MAY 9, 1942

USS Maumee
Baltimore, Maryland
Delbert

Dear Folks,

I took the train from Des Moines to the Philadelphia Navy Yard. There are a good three-to-four hundred sailors here. There's some Limeys and soldiers at the recreation center all sitting around tables drinking beer and milk and eating ice-cream. There's quite a rumble of voices all around. Every so often someone will get up to play "Deep in the Heart of Texas," or some other familiar number on the piano. We all get a kick out of it and clap. The ones who have had six or eight pitchers of beer really get a kick out of it! The rest of us have fun just watching them.

Have you got all the corn planted? I suppose you'll get the plowing job now, Junior! Take it easy with that tractor and don't get to thinking you are a hot driver!

How's the chickens coming along, Mom? Have Dan or Junior get your picture with them.

I'm assigned to the USS Maumee, an oil tanker at Baltimore, Maryland. Our equipment is fine [censored out] like an [censored out] pull trigger, but sure have enough on here to put up a "steel welcome" sign if we get a chance to use them.

They put out an order the other day about censored mail. We're told to keep our letters to love, kisses, and our health. If the censor won't pass it, they'll send it back to me. Several of the fellows here got theirs back. There is just so much going on up and down this coast that they have to watch every possible angle.

Can you send the addresses of Grandmother and my aunts and uncles? The more letters I get, the better I feel. You should see my shipmates as they stand around with that look in their eye as the mail call sounds—especially the seventeen-year-olds.

Well, all of you keep your chins up and don't work too hard.

Delbert

When the Wilsons received the letter from Delbert, they were well aware that U-boat wolf packs were targeting tankers all along the East Coast.

CHAPTER 3

Summer 1942

Dallas County, Iowa
Summer 1942
Clabe

Dear Delbert –

Dan has got all the corn all plowed over once and some of it twice. He is going to help Junior and me put up hay for a few days. He sure can plow corn in a hurry with that tractor.

I've got a new rod and reel I'd like to try out this fall. By that time the squirrels should be about ripe. You know how we always look forward to that hunting season. I don't know that I will ever outgrow that and the old Winchester.

Dad

Along with the letter, Clabe sent his son snapshots from home, including one of Leora with her chickens. Delbert read his dad's words and thought about how each of his brothers had received his own gun at the age of twelve. His dad taught them all to shoot and how to be careful handling guns. During the Depression, Clabe taught all the boys how to dress rabbits and squirrels to feed the family. They trapped fur animals for a little income as well.

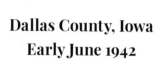

Dallas County, Iowa
Early June 1942

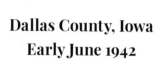

Dale came jogging up the hollyhock-lined driveway. While preparing for the Air Force, Dale was not farming with his dad and brothers, but rather helping his mother pick pans full of Senator Dunlap strawberries. He made the half-mile hike to the main road where their mailbox was and returned with Spats trotting alongside.

"It's a letter from Don!"

Leora had the windows open, enjoying a pair of mourning doves call back and forth, while stemming strawberries. Hearing Dale's shout, she left her pan and stuck her head out the back door. "What date is on it?"

Donald usually wrote home about once a week, but they hadn't heard from him for almost a month. The radio news told about skirmishes around different islands in the Pacific, so the Wilsons were concerned. One of those battles was in the Coral Seal.

"Postmarked May 27."

"Oh, thank God! What a relief to know he's okay after that battle. Here, come in and let's read it."

Donald

Dear Folks,

In good health, kicking along as usual. Has Dale passed his tests for the Air Corps? Has Delbert left for the Navy?

I suppose all of you folks listen to your radio and read the papers, of course. There seems to be a lot of propaganda broadcasts picked up in the states. I hope none of you pay any attention to it. If they are not confirmed, or until the news is, you need not pay much attention to it at all. It's just another weapon, that's all.

Donald

"Well that's what I suspected." Dale folded the letter and tucked it back into the envelope. "I'm sure glad he is safe."

Dale and Leora heard Junior's warbled whistle come towards the house as Clabe, Danny, and Junior were on their way in from the fields. They couldn't wait to share the letter.

"News from Don," Leora shared as she poured warm water from the wood stove's reservoir into an enamel wash pan on the back porch.

"When did he write it?" Danny too was worried about his brother and the Coral Sea Battle. After finding out it was after that, he asked if Don was okay.

"You know Donald," Leora said. "He always says he's kicking along okay."

Besides strawberries, Leora and Dale had harvested a dishpan full of fresh leaf lettuce, all that they could eat. "That's all I want for dinner!" Junior exclaimed. "A big bowl of lettuce washed down with milk from the cow." They all laughed at Junior and were light-hearted about the news from Donald.

Leora

Leora canned extra strawberries in quart jars to be enjoyed in the winter. The canning process meant keeping the stove hot, even in the sultry weather. It wasn't uncommon for Iowa summers to reach 100 degrees. The Minburn house had no electricity, so Leora made do, even without a fan.

Darlene and Sam came over every couple of weeks from rural Madison County. Clabe and Sam liked to do a little fishing in the river across the road during their visits.

One Saturday when Darlene and Sam were there, Dale mentioned going to Perry to pick up a list of items he would need to take to the Air Force. Leora decided to go along so she could market her eggs. Darlene wanted to visit Doris while in Perry. They all made a day of it.

When they arrived in Perry, Doris had her things packed and ready to move. "Why are you moving?" Darlene asked.

"My landlord has been called to the service and his wife is moving too. Do you think Sam will be drafted?"

"We really don't know yet. So far, they want the farmers to keep on farming. Now, with a baby on the way, I hope he won't have to," Darlene said. "If he's called up, I'll just go home and stay with the folks."

"I'm so glad Donald is okay," Doris said.

"He is lucky," responded Leora. "I told him to write often, even if it's only a little and he can't say much. I just want to know that he's okay. Doris, when will you get to come home next?"

"Whenever Dale leaves, if I can. I hate that I didn't get to see Delbert off."

"Soon we are going to have three boys to write to," Leora said. "Danny just turned nineteen and is about to register for the draft. Clabe says we'll have to quit the big farming if Dan is taken to war."

"The landlord has too much land for just Dad and Junior to take care of," Dale remarked.

Leora thought about what would happen if it came to that. She would have to take dinner out to them while they worked the north farm. It was too far away for them to come home in the middle of the day.

"Are you still thinking about getting a smaller place?" asked Doris.

"An acreage or something, we hope by next year."

That was Leora's fondest hope for the family—a place of their own. And for the family to all be safe and together again.

Dallas County, Iowa
Mid-June 1942

Clabe and his sons trooped inside for dinner after scraping off their work shoes by the back door and wiping them clean on an old rug. "The hay is too wet," Clabe told Leora as he washed up. It had rained during the night.

Leora had been up late the night before making sure all the peas were sealed. She canned eleven quarts, but the last one didn't make that "thunk" sound the lids made when they were sealed until around midnight.

Clabe continued, "We've got the south barn more than half full, but it will have to dry down some before we can put the rest in."

"Let's hear the noon news." Danny adjusted the knobs on the big radio. Leora dished up pork chops, creamed peas, and a big bowl of leaf lettuce. Junior poured glasses of milk as the family listened to the news coming in about the Pacific.

"Sounds like American troops on that Midway Island have had a battle," Danny said. "Isn't that where Delbert sent a picture of himself with an albatross a few years ago? When he was in the Navy the first time?"

"I believe it was," Clabe said. "It's not near the Coral Sea, is it? If Don's ship was in the Coral Sea, surely it won't be in the action up there, do you think?"

"Let's just pray that it isn't," Leora said.

A few days later, Clabe needed Prince Albert tobacco. Leora rode along to town with him to sell more eggs at the market. The front-page headlines of one of the newspapers reported a U.S. carrier was hit in a battle at Midway, so they brought home a copy.

Later that evening, Clabe, drawing in on his pipe, said, "It looks like we had some planes damaged and some lost."

"Does it say land based or carrier planes?" Danny wanted to know.

"It doesn't tell which, but says American casualties were light."

The Wilsons hated learning the USS *Lexington*, another aircraft carrier, had been lost at Coral Sea the month before, and that a carrier had been damaged just off Midway Island.

"My, I hope we hear from Donald-boy again soon," said Leora.

The family kept busy with field work and chores. Every day they hiked or drove the half mile dirt road to the main road, anxiously checking the mailbox, hoping to get word from Donald. How thankful they were to finally receive one from him postmarked June 11. It was written in pencil this time.

U.S.S. Yorktown, E-Div.
c/o Fleet P.M., San Francisco, California
June 10, 1942

Donald W. Wilson

Dear Folks,

I'm okay and in good health. I figure you listen to the radio and read the papers, so you know the Japs caught hell in the North Pacific. I guess they know if you're gonna dish it out, you've got to take it. I'd like Dale to realize that, and if he's a pilot in the Air Corps in the near future, he needs to know he's fighting an able enemy. He can be beaten.

Donald

A few days later Danny and Spats came running and hollering up the dirt road with another letter from Don. They learned that Donald was on another ship.

Donald

Dear Folks,

It sure was a surprise, but this letter is to let you know that I'm transferred to the U.S.S. California and my address is changed. I'm getting squared away on here alright. Don't exactly know what job I will have, though it doesn't make a whole lot of difference to me.

Donald

The Wilsons were puzzled to find out that Don had been transferred to an old battleship. "Too bad everything is censored," Junior piped up. "Bet he has quite a story to tell."

Delbert

Dear Don,

Just got the news. Quite a surprise that you got transferred. How did you do it? Whatever you said in your letter to me was clipped out by the censor. Write and give me the dope!

Delbert

Rural Minburn
Dallas County, Iowa
June 1942

With the United States declaring war on Bulgaria, Hungary, and Romania, radio news about the war was a constant backdrop on the farm.

About a month after Delbert reenlisted, it was Dale's turn to pack his bags for the war. On the morning he was to leave, he came down the stairs with his small suitcase packed with what the Air Corps recommended.

"Breakfast is about ready," his mother told him. Clabe, and brothers Danny and Junior were washing up from their morning chores. "Dale boy, I'm sure going to miss your help in the garden," Leora said as she patted him on the arm.

"I'm going to miss helping, too. Mom, you work too hard. Maybe Doris can help out some during the summer."

"I sure can, on my days off." Doris was home to see Dale off and wish him good luck.

"Darlene could too, but your twin has her own garden to tend and now a baby to prepare for."

"Darlene does have her hands full." Dale scooped up a helping of scrambled eggs and a slice of bread. "Dad, do you think you, Danny, and Junior can keep up with the farm work?"

Clabe shoved his chair back from the table, reached for a container of Prince Albert and his pipe. "Well if we can't, the landlord will just have to get us some help." After filling the pipe with tobacco, he lit it and began to draw on the stem.

"He might have to sell some livestock," Junior chimed in.

"That would help," agreed Danny. "Finding a place of our own would be even better, especially if my draft number comes up soon."

"I need to get changed," Leora said. "Doris, could you take care of the dishes?"

"Sure, Mom. Maybe while we are in Des Moines we can find a service flag."

When everyone was cleaned up and ready, they paused in the driveway long enough for a photo. Spats sniffed each one in their best clothes. Clabe wore a suit and hat. Junior had his hair neatly combed, wore slacks and a shirt and stood with his feet apart and arms akimbo. Leora wore a printed dress and hat. Danny and Dale wore their suits, shirts with open collars, and had their hair slicked back.

CLABE, JUNIOR, LEORA, DANNY, DALE. MINBURN, JUNE 8, 1942

"You two look like twins!" Doris held her Brownie camera, waiting for them to line up. "Dale, with your determination, you're sure to make a good pilot."

"I'm gonna try my darndest. This is my chance to learn something besides farming."

Dale drove them all in the Plymouth to Des Moines for the swearing in at the Old Federal Building. The Army Air Force had urged men ages eighteen to twenty-six to become pilots, mechanics, navigators, and bombardiers. Dale's long-time dream of learning to fly was going to become a reality. As a boy, he had carved wooden planes for a school exhibition. He got into trouble for drawing airplanes on his school work, and of course there was that ride in a bi-plane with his younger brothers.

Dale turned over the car keys to Danny. Before the family returned to the farm, Doris helped her mother look for a service flag with three stars for their farmhouse window, but they had no luck.

Three brothers in the service was unusual this early in the war. "I may have to borrow the service flag my own mother used twenty-four years ago," Leora said. Three of her brothers were drafted in the so-called "war to end all wars." Now she had three boys of her own, and even her younger brothers who were involved in war work. "Doris, did I tell you that your Uncle Clarence is working at a bomber plant in Omaha?"

"No. What will he do with his furnace company?"

"I think just men who can fix them will still work there, but they have no new ones to sell. Grandmother also said that your Uncle Willis is doing some kind of defense work out in California. This war is even upsetting things out there."

"I sure hope it's all over soon," Clabe sighed. Everyone nodded in agreement.

Junior, who was almost eighteen, got his first driver's license while in Des Moines.

The next morning, Spats, who was allowed in the house only as far as the kitchen, greeted each of them, but waited at the bottom of the stairs for Dale to come down. According to Danny, Spats acted different all day, sensing that Dale was missing.

Now with three sons to write to, Leora encouraged the brothers to write to each other. Delbert and Donald both wrote encouraging letters to Dale, saying he would make one of the best there was in the Air Force. "And we're all pullin' for you."

Clabe

Having only an eighth-grade education, Clabe claimed he wasn't much of a letter writer. But he wrote a letter to Donald after Dale had left for the Corps and told about what was going on at the farm.

Dear Don,

There's a lot going on here on the farm. If Danny gets a draft notice, we might soon be out of the big farming business. Thirty acres of hay, eighty of corn, seventy of oats and thirty of soybeans is a lot to handle with just two sons home. Not to mention the pigs, cattle, horses, and mules. The boss might have to buy us some more equipment to get it all done. We have about all we can handle now without you, Delbert, and Dale.

We're still thinking of finding an acreage of our own where your mom can keep her chickens and have a garden.

We were sure glad to hear from you with all the news going on. Keep writing.

Dad

Santa Ana Army Air Base, Southern California
Summer, 1942
Dale

Dale had scarcely been out of Iowa his whole life. He had been to Grandmother Goff's in Omaha, and once he did field work in Minnesota. This was his first train ride, and it was a long one. He was sent to Santa Ana Army Air Base in Southern California via Denver and Salt Lake City. The base was a beehive of more than 10,000 cadets from all over the United States.

Dear Mom and Dad,

This place is a hotbed of rumors! There are pilots washing out from training, bitter disappointment, and ending up in bombardier, navigator, or ground crew schools. Only a few from each class will actually get to be pilots. I know some who already have a civilian pilot's license and plenty of flying hours who didn't make it. It is hard to believe that I will have to fly solo after just eight hours of instruction.

We are told that we could be washed out from fainting or getting dizzy from inoculations. If I'm lucky enough to get classified as a pilot, I will certainly be on top of the world. Most of us have a slim chance, but I'm going to work like hell for it. If I fail that, then navigator will be my next try, then bombardier, then mechanic. I ought to get one of those jobs.

I'll have to complete three stages of training if I'm going to earn my pilot's wings. Primary is first. I'll take off and land a small plane, probably a Stearman biplane, and complete turns, glides and stalls. I'm also study-ing weather, aircraft, and engines.

If I survive Primary, I'll be in Basic Training at another base. I'll get seventy more hours of flight training in a larger, low-wing plane with an enclosed cockpit and several instruments. There will be a lot of classroom training there as well.

If I don't wash out by then, I'll be in Advanced Training. This is where they assign either single or multi-engine planes. This is also where I find out what I'll end up flying in combat.

Well, things are going to start and be pretty fast and furious. I'm going to like it, I think. Get in the blue "Zoot Suit," the harness of a parachute, keen goggles, the feel of the stick and plane, and look down over the side of the cockpit. . . Boy, I hope things fit my imagination! Ha!

They sure keep us busy here. Everything is so interesting, and I hardly even have time to get homesick. Sometimes I do a little. But when I get in that plane, I'll think of Danny and what he would think if I washed out! That makes me try all the harder!

Mom, don't you work too hard and try and pick all those beans yourself.

Love and good luck to you all,

Cadet Dale R. Wilson

Dale had described just about everything he could in his letter home, knowing that Dan and Junior were also thinking about trying for cadet when they were old enough. He told them about the pressure chamber and working his jaw to equalize the pressure on his eardrums while it simulated coming back to earth.

He did, in fact, enjoy the academic portion of all his training. Morse Code took a lot of practice, but he likened it to learning to type. After a while the "dits and dahs" went into the ears and out the pencil. In one of the letters home, he wrote the entire alphabet in code so his brothers could practice.

Dale's letters were upbeat and full of anticipation. Leora was glad for that. But she still hoped Dale would not have to see combat.

Perry, Iowa
Summer, 1942
Doris

McDonald Drug sold Evening in Paris Cologne, which shoppers could sense as soon as they entered the store. Whenever any of the Wilsons were in Perry to shop or sell eggs, they honked their "party line" phone ring—long, short, long—near the store so Doris would know they were in town. During her break, dressed in a gold uniform, white apron, saddle shoes with seamed-silk hose, hair in a snood-covered pageboy, Doris would join them in the Plymouth to read the latest letters from her brothers.

She also wrote letters during her breaks.

Dear Donald,

Mom brought your letter in for me to read. She also brought Dale's, so I've been keeping up on the family news from home. I suppose you couldn't explain about your move to the California, but we all have good imaginations. Maybe too good!

I just went to a dance at Lake Robbins, a ballroom near Woodward. We are going out next Wednesday night, too. I don't know whether we will go out for the fourth or not. I may have to work. Cab Calloway plays. I imagine it will be too crowded and too much "hi-de-ho," anyway.

I've been roller skating once or twice since you've been away. I don't drive though, so I'm hoping to get Danny and Junior to start skating so one of them can drive and we could go to Boone more often. A fellow plays the Hammond electric organ and it is just perfect to skate with. It's a brand-new Roller Palace and boy, do they ever have crowds!

Well, people are starting to come in and my break is almost over. So long and good luck!

Doris

Doris also wrote to another cadet at the Santa Ana base. Warren Neal, a farmer who was in the class ahead of Doris at Dexter, had joined the Army Air Force a month before Dale. She had dated Warren some since high school. Francis Love, a classmate of Doris's, was also at Santa Ana, but with 10,000 cadets there, Dale probably wouldn't get a chance to see either of them.

The WAACs, the women's branch of the US Army, had been created that May. Doris thought about joining but admitted to Delbert that she didn't like the idea of not knowing for sure where she'd be sent. Delbert answered that he thought the WAVES was the best military organization for women. "As far as being wild and rough, you'll find that everywhere you go. War makes it worse, of course. You'll find good shipmates and bad." Delbert told her to keep their folks and the boys cheered up. "You never realized it, but you always had that effect on me whenever you came home."

Doris went home about every other weekend. Darlene and her husband got over home about that often, too. Since there was a phone at the farmhouse, she'd just call when she arrived at the depot for a ride home.

One time when she got to Minburn, no one was home when she tried to call. She started walking the two miles to the farm. Soon after starting, a neighbor drove by and picked her up. "Your folks went to a movie this evening," he told her. "I heard the long-short-long ring and figured it was you trying to get ahold of them."

When Doris was home, not only did she help her mother with gardening and canning, they also did the laundry and ironing together. Doris got her own laundry done that way, too.

Once she brought home a ceramic cat and set it on the buffet where she'd been dusting. There were shotgun shells on the buffet, left when her brothers had been cleaning their guns, so she opened a top drawer and raked the shells into it. They'd left the guns leaning against the buffet, which was no place for them, so she carried them to the back porch and continued cleaning.

"Hey, you can't do that!" Danny found the guns. "You'll leave fingerprints all over them and they'll rust."

"Well then, if you put them where they belong, I won't touch them."

Danny headed to the buffet for the shells but stopped in his tracks. "Get a gun!" he shouted. He had spotted the ceramic cat. "Where did that come from?"

"Oh, it was just a gift. Say, could you take me back to Perry?"

"Sure," Danny said. "But I'll have to change out of these greasy overalls." He was always working on farm machinery.

While Danny changed, Doris decided to back the Plymouth out of the garage. She turned the steering wheel too soon, hit the side of the garage, and bent the fender. With a red face, she admitted what she'd done. The fender was crushed against a tire.

Danny, who liked things neat and just so, shook his head when he saw it. "I'm not driving you. Everyone will think *I* did that." And he meant it.

"How will I get back to my job?" Doris asked.

Junior didn't get the chance to drive the car much, so he was delighted to volunteer. He tugged on the fender to pull it away from the tire so it wouldn't rub and happily drove Doris back to Perry.

The next time Doris was home, she checked the car's fender and noted that it hadn't been fixed yet.

"You know, Danny, if it had a new chrome strip, the car would be like new."

"Chrome is one of the things we can't get until the war is over," Danny reminded her. This made her feel worse about the accident.

"I'm sure sorry about it. No more backing out the car until I've got someone to teach me."

"And I'm sorry I let you suffer a little." Danny grinned. "We already have the replacement. We've just been too busy to put it on."

LEORA, DANNY ON TRACTOR, JUNIOR.
CULTIVATING CORN. SUMMER 1942

Rural Minburn
Summer, 1942
Clabe and Leora

Dressed in clean overalls, Clabe drove into Adel to sell some hogs. While there, he noticed the headlines in *The Perry Daily Chief*: "Aircraft Carrier Yorktown Receives Direct Hit at Midway."

This was the first time the *Yorktown* had been named. He bought a copy to take home. He also picked up a Des Moines newspaper.

As Clabe neared the house, Spats announced that he was driving up the lane. Clabe hurried into the house to share the news with Leora.

"Leora, there's pictures of Don's ship in the newspaper!"

Busy cutting up plums to can, she wiped her hands on her apron. "Let me see. Oh my! There's half a page of smoke and planes. This is his ship?"

"Yes, it even names the *Yorktown*. I figure that's why they moved him to the *California*," said Clabe. "I sure wish they would let him come home like Harold Snyder did." Harold was a neighbor boy who was in the Coast Guard in New York.

"Harold's folks just got a letter from him," Leora replied. "He said he wasn't sure just when he would be able to come home, then the next day he surprised them. I sure wish Donald could do that, too. Here, let's save a copy of the paper to give to Donald when he does come home."

Leora wrote letters nearly every day. She kept her writing paper, stamps, a bottle of ink, and her favorite fountain pen on the old buffet. She wrote her mother in Omaha, her sister in California, Delbert on the

East Coast, Dale in Southern California, and Donald…well, she wrote to him wherever he was now. They hadn't heard from him in almost four weeks, but she continued to send letters, hoping they would catch up with him.

Dear Donald,

Well, we just read the full story, or what they printed as the full story, of the battle of Midway. We surmised why you were transferred. I guess you "would" tell us your experience "if" you could. I hope that time comes soon.

The news of the battle first came from the Navy over the radio last night on the late news. We didn't hear about it 'til this morning when your dad saw the papers when he was in Adel selling hogs. There was a picture of your ship after the battle. I tell you what, we did a lot of wondering where and how you were and just keep hoping and praying that you are okay. We were sure glad that the last letter we got from you was dated after June fourth.

News is trickling in about another battle in the Pacific. We are hoping and praying everything goes alright with that, too. Makes us pretty anxious, I tell you.

Love,
Mom

Seven months after Pearl Harbor had been attacked, four homes just west of Minburn had already sent eight boys into the military. In July of 1942, *The Dallas County News* called it "Dallas County's most patriotic rural neighborhood."

The Roy Snyders' son, Harold, was in the U.S. Coast Guard in New York City and Marion Brelsford was in California in the U.S. Army.

The Voas family had three sons serving: Darrell, a lieutenant in Wyoming; Hollis in California; and Norris in Missouri.

And three Wilson boys: Donald, serving his ninth year in the Navy, in the Pacific; Delbert, currently in the Atlantic and having earlier served four years; and Dale, an aviation cadet in California.

The article also told about Mrs. Wilson using her mother's three-star flag from the Great War.

Leora's mother, Laura Goff, who was reputed to be able to get more writing on a postcard than anyone, wrote that Leora's brother Rolla was in the Army, and another brother, Perry, was waiting to be called up. Clarence Goff was already in the Navy. "So I had three brothers in World War I," Leora said, "and three brothers in this war."

Leora's brothers survived World War I. Surely her three younger brothers and three sons would survive this one.

LOAD OF HAY.
CLABE, DANNY ON LOAD, JUNIOR ON TRACTOR.
SUMMER 1942

Santa Maria, California
Summer, 1942
Dale

Now classified as an Air Cadet, it was Dale's chance to actually become a pilot. 150 single-engine, PT-13 Stearman bi-wing trainers awaited the 300 cadets at Hancock College of Aeronautics in Santa Maria, California. Dale climbed into one of the planes the first chance that he could to look everything over. Bright blue fuselage with two open cockpits and yellow wings, rudder pedals that were far apart, a throttle that was just right. Dale pronounced the Stearman as "keen."

Dear Mom and Dad,

I went up Thursday afternoon and then again yesterday morning. They were each half-hour rides. The first time up they let you take the controls. We did medium–bank turns, climbs, glides, stalls, and a few coordination exercises. Then the instructor did a right spin. It was fun! Some of the boys got sick and messed up the plane. It didn't affect me any, only a little when we took a quick dive. The second time up I felt a little more at home.

We had four to five hours to learn how to take-off and land the plane. After eight hours we were expected to fly solo. You really have to learn fast or they will wash you. This school has a reputation for being one of the toughest in the country. They have the highest percentage of washouts. But they also have some of the best instructors and turn out the best pilots. The last Squadron that went through had only eighty-eight out of 186 Cadets make it.

I gotta say the chow here is pretty good. Some of the best eatin' in my life. I have all the fruit, vegetables, milk, and buttermilk that I like. I even have my cracked wheat for breakfast with all the rich cream I want, along with whole wheat bread. Can't complain.

As soon as I solo, I'll no longer be considered a gopher. All the upper-classmen here get to shower first after athletics. Gophers have to wait. We also have to do all the cleaning in the barracks. Can't wait till that first solo.

I've been writing to Delbert, Donald, Sam and Darlene, and Doris, so I'm expecting some mail soon. Del wrote back and said to keep up the ol' fight and spirit to win. I hope that my future letters won't be about washing out!

Dale
P.S. Send a picture of Spats.

SPATS, A BRINDLED BULLDOG MIX

Santa Maria, California
August 22, 1942

Dale

Dear Mom and Dad,

I did it! I soloed!

After I got the plane down for a three-point landing, my instructor told me to taxi over the line. I knew what that meant; it was my turn to go solo.

The front of the plane was light without the instructor. I thought I would be nervous and tense up at the controls. As it turns out, I was much calmer flying alone. The landing was the best I had ever made, and my instructor agreed. It sure does make one feel keen and confident. Especially after thirty cadets have washed out this week alone.

Dale

Santa Maria, California
September, 1942
Dale

Dear Mom and Dad,

126 cadets have washed out so far. Four of them were from my barracks. I'm glad this letter isn't about me washing out!

I've gained about 18 pounds since being here. I can feel that I am thicker, and I don't mean fat. Ha! Boy, they sure do serve good chow here.

One of the cadets in our barracks found WHO Des Moines on the radio. He turned it up loud since most of us here are Iowans. Bob Burlingame was giving the 10:15 news. It sounded just like being at home.

Dale

A/C DALE R. WILSON, SANTA MARIA, CALIFORNIA. AUGUST 1942

Minburn, Iowa
September 1942

The summer was another hot and humid one on the Iowa farm. The buzz of locusts, chirp of tree frogs, swooping bats, and hooting owls were the songs of summer in Iowa. The twinkling of fireflies at twilight brought a certain magic to the landscape.

Leora wrote letters after the others had gone to bed. She reported canning 172 quarts of tomato juice and 103 quarts of tomatoes. She wrote of gas rationing and how it was supposed to save rubber. She kept all the boys up with news of life on the farm.

One September evening while she was writing, the phone on the wall rang—long-short-long. She wondered who could be calling this late.

"Hello, this is the Wilsons," Leora greeted when she picked up the line.

"Mom? It's me—Dale!"

"Dale? Where are you? I can hardly hear you."

"Yes, it's me, Mom. I passed!"

"You what? I can't hear you." The line was weak which meant that several neighbors who were on the same party line had heard their ring and were listening in. Eight or nine families were on the same party line as the Wilsons', and some would "rubber," or listen in. They all knew each other's telephone rings. Each receiver off the hook weakened the volume.

The operator, also listening in, asked the others to hang up so Wilsons could hear each other. They did. By then Clabe was standing by the phone.

"Mom, I passed Primary!"

"Good for you, son. We knew you would. Where do you go next?"

"Taft, for Basic. Say, are Danny and Junior up?"

"I'll go get them. Here's your dad." Clabe took the earpiece next while Leora went part way up the stairs to wake the younger brothers.

"Is Dale here?" Junior rubbed his eyes.

"No, but he's on the telephone and wants to talk to you both."

While Danny talked to Dale, Clabe smiled at Leora and Junior. "He waited in line for an hour to use the phone, just to let us know he'd passed."

When Junior took his turn, Danny told the others Dale said they all sounded so clear, like he was right beside them in the room.

Dale later wrote that he'd imagined himself in the kitchen at home, and that it was the most he ever got out of $2.50 in his life.

CHAPTER 4

Autumn 1942

Gardner Field, Taft, California
Autumn, 1942

Dale

Dear Mom and Dad,

Say, it sure was keen talking to you way over there and down by the river. I'm not settled in at Gardner Field. I'm training in the Vultee Valiant BT-13. We call it the "Vultee Vibrator!" It sure is big and when we take off, it really bellers and whines with the propeller in low pitch. It is just like I heard it would be. Like going from a Model T Ford into a big Buick. The ride is smooth and twice as fast as a primary trainer.

I'm catching on quickly. After a little over four hours of training, I got to be the first one to solo. What a thrill that was!

Hey Danny—remember when I told you that my goal is to fly an Airacobra? Well, I'm one notch closer! I got to sit in an Airacobra P-39 and mess around with the controls for about fifteen minutes. It sure is a keen little airplane. The cockpit is just right with a parachute on. There's a 37-mm cannon in the nose, two machine guns in the top of the nose, and two machine guns in each wing. It really is built keen. I hope to fly one of them in a couple of months. A Colonel flew it away one afternoon. Boy it was really traveling. About halfway down the runway, he rocked back on the wheels, raised the nose off the ground and shot up into the sky. He had the landing gear up before he reached 200 feet!

We have a new swimming pool at the base. For the dedication, Johnny Weissmuller, the Tarzan of the movies, did dives and exhibition swimming for everyone.

71

Last week they showed all of us cadets a sex hygiene film. It was just before supper and I sure didn't have a good appetite after that. I guess they wanted the guys to do some thinking before we get out on open post.

I just got a letter that I mailed to Donald sent back to me. It was written before the sinking of the Yorktown. It only took six months to get here! I'm sending it home along with this letter to keep as a souvenir.

When I was on furlough, I went to visit Uncle Willis and Aunt Ann in Los Angeles. We drove to Pasadena with their daughters to visit Uncle Wayne. Mom, your brothers send their greetings.

Dale

A/C DALE R. WILSON, GARDNER FIELD, TAFT,
CALIFORNIA. OCTOBER 1942

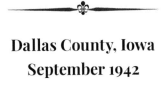

Dallas County, Iowa
September 1942

Donald's ship hadn't just been damaged at Midway, the aircraft carrier *Yorktown* had been completely sunk. The Navy finally announced it over three months after the fact.

In the sweltering Minburn farm kitchen, Darlene and her mother had just filled scalded quart jars with hot tomato juice.

"Do you suppose Donald lost any of his keepsakes?" Darlene wondered.

"Wouldn't be surprised. He was lucky to save himself," Leora said. "My, we sure are a lucky family, aren't we?"

"I hope he'll get home when Dale has his furlough. Wouldn't that be grand?"

"Maybe Delbert could even manage it so he could be here at the same time."

Using hot pads, Darlene screwed a lid onto each jar, wiping the sides with a dish rag. "Did I tell you Sam filled out his Draft Board Questionnaire? He had to tell them about dependents and the kind of farming that he does."

"Do you really think he'll be drafted?" Leora began to lift the jars with a wire bail into a large kettle of boiling water on the stove.

"Well maybe not after the baby arrives. Sam and his dad have been so busy."

"Farmers need to stay home and raise beef for our sailors and soldiers," added Leora.

"Is Doris really going to join the WAACS or WAVES?"

"She sure is talking about it. She and a waitress friend from Perry just got jobs at Bishops Cafeteria in Des Moines." A dozen jars of hot tomato juice filled the kettle, with a couple of inches of simmering water over them. Leora checked the clock. The canning process would take about forty-five minutes.

"If Sam does go in the Army, I'll just come home and help. I wish Doris would too. She'd be good company for you, Mom."

"She says there's no future in being a waitress, but they make more money in Des Moines and the hours are better. I'm just afraid she won't get home as often. Say, Darlene, did I tell you we made the final payment on the Plymouth?"

"That's great! Now you can save the car payment money for that place of your own you and dad have always wanted."

"That's what we hope to do. And I hope this war gets over soon so the boys can all come home for good. That would be the grandest."

Darlene and Leora both sat down and wrote letters to Donald.

LEORA AND HER FLOCK OF CHICKENS, OCTOBER 1942

Dear Donald,

 I've tried to get a letter out to you for some time now. I was waiting to see if Sam could write a little, but he is busy with his dad combining soy beans and picking corn. Guess he's going to wait till after the rush season and our blessed event arrives.

 We are hoping that Sam doesn't get drafted since he's so busy farming and with a baby on the way. If he does, I'll come home and help mom out.

 Miss hearing from you. Hope this letter finds you safe and well.

Darlene

Dear Donald,

 What a lot of stories you must have if you could tell them! We are thankful you are okay. I guess we are a lucky family and I hope it stays that way.

 It helps to get your letters, even if you can't write much. Just a few lines pretty regular would help us to stand this whole thing better. It gives us a lift to hear from you. It would be grand for the war to be over soon and you could tell us about everything.

 I know things are going to be okay. Keep your chin up. We are praying and working for victory to come soon.

Love, Mom

Dallas County, Iowa
September 1942
Junior and Danny

By the end of September, mornings awakened with fog. The sumac at the edge of the timber had begun to turn red. Hawks soared overhead. The Wilsons took a break from farm work to drive to Perry to see "The Battle of Midway" in Technicolor, hoping to see the story of Donald's ship.

Junior wrote to Donald:

Dear Donald,

No doubt you saw plenty of action with the Yorktown. Those Japs are wiry, determined devils, but a mass of slugs will stop them. I'll bet the ack-ack guns were barking plenty. I wouldn't mind being in one of those Grumman Wildcats.

I'm thinking about enlisting in the Navy when I turn 18. I aim not to be drafted. I think the Navy needs a strong back in there. They practically got us all and we'll give the enemy one hell of a battle.

I'm getting fed up with all the pitching of manure on the farm. When the snow melts in the spring, I'm taking up new tactics.

It's squirrel season and I just brought in five fat ones! I could have easily brought in fifteen. When I went hunting with Danny and Spats, we came home with thirteen squirrels. We skinned and dressed them, and mom fried them up with bacon and butter for supper. We'll do some fox hunting this winter. I saw one up the road only about a hundred yards from the house. I could have hit him with a sling shot. Game is plentiful, that's for sure. But hunting won't be as enjoyable this year. We'll get together after the war on this subject, eh?

It's been about a year since you were home. Wish it was so you could come back again for some cornbread and squirrel legs.

Keep your chin up and fighting,

Junior

Danny wrote his version of the story:

Dear Donald,

Junior and I haven't done as much hunting this fall with all the work there is to do. We did go out one afternoon and got 13. There was a squirrel every 50 yards! Duck and pheasant season have been lengthened about a month. There's a lot of pheasants this year with nobody to get them. The open season is on the Japs from now on.

I'm still thinking about joining the Air Corps. They plan to have a two-million-man force, so I ought to have a chance to be one of them. Ha! People are being drafted all over. The Washington Township superintendent is expecting to be drafted and the school is even hiring women as school bus drivers!

Write when you can,

Danny

During the remainder of autumn 1942, Danny and Junior kept busy helping their dad among the hay, manure, the landlord's livestock, and fieldwork. They also studied on their own in order to pass military tests.

Dallas County, Iowa
October 1942

On October 21, 1942, the three Wilson men trooped in for breakfast after morning milking and feeding chores. Leora greeted them with the big news.

"Sam called from the hospital. Richard Wilson Scar was born at 7:00 this morning!"

"Hey," said Junior, "I'm an uncle! And so are you, Danny."

As Leora passed around the scrambled eggs, she went on to say that visiting hours would be in the evening. "Could we get everything done here so we can all go meet little Richard Wilson Scar? Oh, my, don't you just love his name?"

Everyone agreed to hustle with evening chores and get the work done so they could meet the newest member of the family.

When Darlene and the baby were released from the hospital, Leora planned to stay with them a little longer. Doris would come home to help take care of Leora's responsibilities on the farm.

"Don't you boys worry," she said. "You won't go hungry when I'm away!" Leora's gold-flecked brown eyes twinkled as she thought of her first grandchild.

After the birth of baby Richard, the family exchanged many letters keeping everyone updated on the happenings at home. The first letter came from Donald who announced that he had just been promoted to Chief Electrician's Mate.

Leora

Dear Donald,

My, how glad to hear this news and relieved to finally receive your letter! This sure is good news. Hurrah for you making Chief!

I'm staying at Darlene's for a couple of weeks to help take care of the newest member of the family. I'm enjoying every minute.

Stay safe and keep writing!

Mom

Darlene

Dear Donald,

Glad to hear you are Chief! Yes, Mom is here taking care of me and the baby. He sure is quite a boy! The new Grandma sure enjoys it, too! It's right up her alley. Ha! I'm afraid she'll want to take him home with her when she goes, but she'll have to miss him a little 'till we can go over home once in a while. This gas rationing will probably stop that to some extent.

Doris is the "chief chicken raiser" at home while mom is here. I hope she can be home if you can get a leave and we can all be together. Wouldn't it be swell if all three of you could make it home at the same time? I suppose in these times that will be impossible. But everything will come out okay. It's got to.

Darlene

Dale

Dear Darlene,

I'm an uncle! Richard Wilson Scar—that's just swell! Gee, congratulations and everything. I'm sure glad you and little Richard are doing fine. Being my twin sister, I sure do think the world of you. Boy, I'll want to come home for sure this winter sometime and see him. He will be quite a little guy by then!

Dale

Darlene

Dear Dale,

Can't wait 'till you boys can come home and see the baby. He's perfect. He smiles when Mom gives him a bath. Sam calls Mom "grandma" all the time. It seems funny, but she loves it. I still can't believe it's all true yet. We are all getting used to life with a baby. Now that he is here, we cannot imagine life without him.

Darlene

Delbert

Dear Mom and Dad,

I hope you can start looking for a small place of your own. The buildings don't have to be the best; soil and location is really the thing to look for. I'm sending $50 now and you can count on me sending that amount home *every month for as long as the war lasts. When I get a promotion, I'll send more. I don't spend much money here like some of the others. I like milk better than beer! Ha! I'm about like you, Dad. As long as I have my Prince Albert pipe tobacco and plenty of chow, I'm just fine.*

The war is going to be a long, hard pull. The quicker we get a place of our own, the more independence we will all have as a family. Mom, you can still have all of your chickens. Don't you all think it would be better if we had our own place and acreage? If you have to, you could even sell the Plymouth. I know it would be hard to do without a car, but it really isn't a fundamental necessity of life. I'm willing to ride a horse or bike when I get back.

Congratulations to Darlene and Sam on their new baby! Can't wait to see the little guy!

Delbert

RICHARD WILSON SCAR'S FIRST VISIT TO GRANDPA AND
GRANDMA WILSON'S. NOVEMBER 15, 1942, MINBURN

Gardner Field, Taft, California
November 1942

Dale

Dear Mom and Dad,

It's near the end of training here. Ten more cadets washed out. I'm glad I wasn't one of them. We were supposed to choose if we wanted to go on to pursuit or bombardment training. I hoped to be sent to pursuit training in the fighter planes next. Those planes are really maneuverable. But I didn't get the news I wanted. I'll be heading to Roswell, New Mexico for twin-engine training school.

That wasn't what I wanted to hear. My only hope now is a P-38 twin-engine, twin-boom fighter plane called the Lightning. I suppose this training is probably more worth it in the long run since flying after the war will mostly be multiple-engine planes. I'm going to keep putting in for pursuit and maybe I'll end up in a P-38. I'd sure like that.

Dale

Dallas County, Iowa
November, 1942

Donald

Dear Mom and Dad,

The USS California is limping along at only ten knots. Instead of four propellers, we have two. We are some real submarine bait if you know what I mean.

You asked me if I lost my keepsakes. I did. I lost everything but my hide. I had them all wrapped and ready to mail home, but I didn't get the time to do it.

I sure would like to get back to Iowa even for a short while. I miss Iowa's fall weather. Tell Dan and Junior to write and let me know how the farming is going and their latest hunting stories. I wish I could be there to get in on the bird season and have some of mom's chicken.

Lately, I've been doing a whole lot of nothing. I go ashore mostly, sleep, eat, and yes…drink. I got pie-eyed on those first couple of liberties! But it sure did relieve the tension.

I asked for seven days' leave and I hope it's approved. Let me know if Doris is still working in Des Moines. If I get the time home, I'll stop there a while. Maybe she can get off work a few days and come home with me.

Tell Junior to get the hunting equipment gathered and be ready to spend a couple of days in the woods. We'll hunt anything that gets up!

Hope to have good news soon.

Donald

❧

Donald was able to come home on leave. Clabe and his younger sons had worked hard to get the corn out of the field so they could really enjoy Donald's visit. They still had regular morning and evening chores to do, but getting the corn out gave them a lot more time during the day.

"You get your things settled upstairs," his mother told Don. "I'll get some joe ready for you. And some pumpkin pudding with whipped cream. How does that sound?" Leora cooked things as simply as possible. With all of her other chores and the letter writing, she skipped making pie crust. They all thought the filling was the best part anyway.

"Sounds great, Mom. It sure is good to be home."

"You sure are a lucky boy, Donald. Losing your ship like that, we were sure worried."

"You know, I served on the *Yorktown* all her life. I'll tell the rest when Dad and the boys get back in."

Soon they heard Spats barking, alerting them both that the others wouldn't be far behind. Don's dad and brothers cleaned up using the wash pan on the porch and joined Leora and Donald at the big kitchen table. Donald began his story.

"I don't think I told you that I had to abandon ship twice. It was about a month after taking a bomb in the Coral Sea, where we lost the *Lexington*. In fact, we were still being repaired at Pearl Harbor when the alert came about Midway. When we got there, dive bombers hit us three times right away, crippling our boilers. We were just getting back in action when I heard something I'd never heard before. We were slammed by a torpedo."

"What was it like?" asked Danny.

"The whole ship rocked! The alarms blared right away and everything went dark. We grabbed flashlights and rushed up flight after flight of stairs like we had trained. We had just grabbed life jackets when we got the signal to abandon ship. I ran to the fantail and jumped."

"Wow, then how were you rescued?" Junior asked.

"There were several ships with us, although there were more alarms once more Jap planes showed up. Men from one of the ships pulled me out of the oily water after about an hour. Wow, I was tired."

"Did the ship sink right away?"

"No. In fact, the next day they decided to try to salvage her. I volunteered for it. That ship was so spooky! It was so quiet without any motors running. I ran down to my battle station for tools. We were using pumps from a destroyer right beside us. It was stifling down there without fans."

Leora brought another pot of hot coffee and passed around bowls of pumpkin pudding.

"The destroyer beside us sent over sandwiches and coffee, so I went topside for some fresh air and food. That's when the GQ alarm started to blare! I jumped up in time to see a torpedo spread headed right towards us! I knew we were doomed. The ship beside us began to sink right away. Loose gear scraped and banged. I headed for the fantail, the same spot where I'd jumped just two days earlier. I leaped down into the elevator pit and scrambled out the other side and went over the side.

"I was rescued again, only quicker this time. The *Yorktown* still didn't sink, but she settled deeper. I fell asleep on the deck of the rescue ship, near the engine room. Someone nudged me awake the next morning in time to stand at attention when she rolled over and sank. Her flags were still flying."

"No wonder you weren't able to save anything. We are just glad you are okay."

"I've certainly learned to appreciate the simple things in life. Now, who's all going hunting?"

Donald, Danny, and Junior hiked through the crisp leaves up the North 'Coon River. They shot some rabbits, pheasants, a duck, a quail, and even a couple of fat squirrels. Their bonanza would provide meals for a couple of days.

While hunting, Donald opened up some more with his brothers.

"I didn't tell the folks, but before I abandoned ship that last time, when more sailors joined me on the stern ready to jump, for some reason I can't explain, I shouted for them to wait. There was a loud explosion under the water, probably depth charges from the destroyer sinking next to us. It churned bodies of the boys already in the ocean. Then we jumped."

"You've seen enough war," said Danny. "The folks, well all of us, will certainly be glad when it's all over."

Before Donald left to go back to Washington State, he had his picture taken at Edmonson's Studio in Perry. He wore his new, dark, double-breasted Chief's uniform with three ribbons to mark his naval service.

He also received letters from Seattle with hearts on them from a girl named Rose.

CEM Donald W. Wilson, Perry, Iowa, November 1942

Dallas County, Iowa
Winter, 1942
Dale

Clabe

Dear Dale,

Dan saws wood, studies, and hunts a little. There have been several wolves around here this winter. The boys and I are going after them the first new snow. We'll have to go easy on the shotgun shells because they aren't making anymore until we get Hitler and Hirohito licked.

Dad

Junior

Dear Dale,

How's the flying going? I'll bet the Cessnas are pretty keen, all right. There's not really much news around here. The usual chopping ice out of the water trough, pitching hay to the old bony cows, and cussing the gray mare every time she's in view. Ha!

I'm thinking about going into flying, too. Either the Army or Navy. I want to enlist before my next birthday, but only the Navy takes seventeen-year-olds.

Hey, a twin-engine job went flying over yesterday. It had plenty of speed and really bellowed!

Everyone is saying that we have to fight to get Hitler first and then the Japs, but I think that is a mistake. Those Japs are going to be our hardest battle. It's going to take all the men the U.S. can produce to whip them, and that includes me.

Junior

Danny

Dear Dale,

Word is that the Allies are on the offensive on all war fronts now. The Red army has pushed the Germans back and claim to have twenty-two divisions circling Stalingrad. The British Eighth Army has Rommel running nearly through Libya, and the Americans and Australians captured a couple of towns in New Guinea.

Hope I'm not too optimistic about all of that.

Danny

Donald

Dear Dale,

It's official. All of my brothers are taller and heavier than me now. I guess I'm the runt of the family! Ha! You will be surprised to see how much Junior has grown this last year. I know I was!

Donald

Bremerton, Washington
Winter, 1942
Donald

After Donald returned to the West Coast, he sent home a citation signed by U.S. Navy Admiral C.W. Nimitz for being among the salvage crew on the flat-top:

United States Pacific Fleet
Flagship of the Commander-in-Chief
The Commander in Chief, United States Pacific Fleet,
takes pleasure in commending
Donald W. Wilson, Electrician's Mate First Class
U.S. Navy
For service set forth in the following

CITATION:

For heroic conduct and meritorious service in the line of his profession as a member of the volunteer salvage crew which attempted on June 6, 1942, to salvage and return the U.S.S. Yorktown to port. Knowing full well that the Yorktown was in a precarious condition of damage received in battle on June 5 [sic], 1942, that she was barely seaworthy, and that she would probably be the target of repeated submarine and air attack against which it would be difficult to defend her, he requested that he be allowed to return to the ship and assist in her salvage. The efforts of the salvage party were so successful that all remaining fires were out, and two degrees of list had been removed when, in mid-afternoon, the ship was struck by two torpedoes fired from an enemy submarine. His conduct was in accordance with the best traditions of the naval services.

C.W. Nimitz
Admiral, U.S. Navy

Dallas County, Iowa
December 1942

As 1942 drew to a close, Leora received a bottle of Jet perfume from Dale for her December 4 birthday. The accompanying letter was enclosed with a Roswell Army Flying School Christmas card with pilot's wings embossed on the holiday scene. Leora wrote Dale to thank him and to catch him up on the happenings in and around the Minburn farm.

Leora

Dear Dale,

Thank you so much for the birthday gift. It arrived on my birthday and I gave it a try right away. I really love it. I think I will keep it in my box of handkerchiefs so they will all smell nice. My collection of embroidered hankies and tatted lace is growing as my mother sends me one every year. How nice that they will all smell wonderful when I pull one out to take with me.

You know, we are just so proud of you, Dale. You are doing a fine job and know you are always doing your best. I think you are going to like the twin-engine school even better than the single. Delbert and the boys say the double engines are better protected in combat.

Speaking of Delbert, we haven't heard from him in over a month. I suppose he is okay. Must be on a long trip. I hope we hear from him soon.

Your dad and the boys have been sorting hogs and getting calves ready for the vet. Last week we went to see the John Wayne movie "Flying

Tigers." *It's about the volunteer aviators who flew on behalf of the Chinese against Japan before Pearl Harbor was attacked. They always show newsreels of the war before the start of movies now.*

It's been a year since the attack on Pearl Harbor and they finally released the information of just how much damage the Japanese had done during the assault. All the ships and lives lost…makes everybody just want to wipe every Jap off the face of the earth. The entire story is in this week's Sunday paper. There are so many pictures of the ships and battleships that were damaged or sunk. Don's battleship was one of them.

Love, Mom

Dear Dale,

Sam was required to send a report of crop acres he plans to farm next year. We still don't think he will be drafted.

It's okay if you are too busy to write a lot of letters. Just send any you can to the folks, and we will read them when we visit. This war has been pretty hard on Mom and Dad. When Don came home, they sure hated to see him go. It was such a short time that he could stay. But it was good for them just to know that Don was safe.

Merry Christmas. We are always thinking of you and rootin' for you. We hope your luck continues. We know it will. Soon you'll be sporting a pair of silver wings!

Darlene

On Christmas Eve, Doris rode the M & St. L train home from Des Moines. After the farm chores were done on Christmas Day, the Wilsons all drove over to Darlene and Sam's near Earlham. Leora stayed with baby Richard while the rest spent the day ice skating. Even Clabe!

That evening back at the Minburn farm, the family listened to Bob Burns on the radio, and Spike Jones and his City Slickers. Bob Hope's WAAC headquarters show was broadcast from Fort Des Moines.

Doris wrote to Delbert.

Dear Delbert,

When I get home to the farm, the first thing I do is sit down and read letters from all of you boys. For about three months now we haven't had any from you, and you can bet we are all getting pretty uneasy. Of course we don't talk to each other about being worried but just the same I can't help but feel it in everyone at home. God, I hope you are OK.

Doris

That year, Doris also received a Christmas card from an air cadet postmarked from Marfa, Texas. It was signed, "With love, Warren." Warren Neal had been a grade ahead of Doris at Dexter High School. After graduation, he farmed with his father and brother until the war started.

Just after Christmas, a letter arrived at the farm from Donald.

Dear Mom and Dad,

Well, it's Christmas Day and I've duty on board. I just finished a hearty Christmas dinner. Trying to settle it now!

I've been spending time going over to the big city pretty regular now. I guess you can figure out why! Trying to figure out if it's "love." If it's not love, then it's something not far from it. We almost decided to get married but thought it would be better to wait until after the war. The "here today, gone tomorrow" lifestyle isn't good for a marriage. And you know I like to travel too much to stay put. It's a hard decision to face. I think I'd rather go into battle than decide!

Don

The year in Iowa ended under a glare of ice after two days of rain on top of snow. Clabe and Junior slid into a ditch with the tractor and it took two hours to get it out. They vowed to leave it in the shed until the weather got better. But they still had livestock to feed, so Leora had plenty of muddy overalls to wash. In the winter, she hung the laundry in the house to dry.

By the end of 1942, Donald was in Bremerton, Washington, assigned to help refit the U.S.S. *California*. Doris lived in Des Moines and worked at Bishops Cafeteria. Darlene was busy with two-month-old Richard. Dale was in Advanced training in Roswell, New Mexico. Danny was waiting for his call to the Army Air Corps. Junior was waiting until he was old enough to join up.

But where was Delbert?

CHAPTER 5

Early 1943

Norfolk, Virginia
January 1943
Delbert

A letter from Delbert finally arrived in mid-January 1943.

Dear Mom and Dad,

I'm finally back in the good ol' U.S.A. after over two months of plowing the Atlantic. It was a bit rough with very poor submarine weather. But we didn't mind it too much as long as we could stay on our feet...most of the time! We reported (unofficially, of course) going 457 miles in one day—57 ahead and 400 up and down. It took us 19 days to get back because of the storm.

We had four destroyers escorting us. They sunk four or five U-boats on the way over, making the dreary Atlantic much safer. The destroyers remind me of a bunch of hound dogs after a fox, smelling and tracking around just like dogs! Their new detection gear could spot anything above or below the waterline.

Our ship mothered about 30 small aircraft, PC boats, sub-chasers, and mine sweeps. We traveled across the Atlantic via Bermuda and the Azores. When we arrived at Casablanca, the Americans on shore thought we looked like an old hen with a bunch of baby chickens! Ha!

I'll give you a clue as to where we had to go so fast. In fact, we left so fast I just about didn't get that last letter off to you. Here's the hint: I'm sorry to say I didn't have the opportunity of meeting Field Marshal Erwin Rommel and his Africa Corps. Just as well. I guess he still has plenty of fight in him.

We approached North Africa and at a range of 10-12 miles, our Navy opened up against a force of shore batteries, French battleships, cruisers, and destroyers. The Jean Bart and cruisers tried very hard to get our big battleship, but their range was a bit short. Then we steamed in so their projectiles would hit the water over us. Our forces dodged about blasting the hell out of everything in sight. We lost most of our men when the landing was made, more than they want to tell us right now.

Before our convoy arrived, a bomb had put the pride of the French Fleet, the Jean Bart, out of action. I had a good view of ships with gaping holes in the sides and the keels on the bottom. Some ships were on their sides and had raging fires. At least a half a dozen Nazi U-boats were sunk. We were anchored inside the backwater for almost a month.

While anchored, I had been on patrol duty. I carried a club and a .45 caliber handgun. Arab kids followed me around doing all sorts of handsprings and tricks for a cigarette or a stick of gum. They were only about six or seven, but worldly-wise at such a young age. Their heads were shaved, all but a half-dollar sized spot on the back of their heads where their hair grew long enough to braid. Now there's a hairstyle!

We had to wait for enough ships to escort us back to the U.S. The Atlantic sure is a wide old pond when you poke along at eight or nine knots. It wasn't until after Christmas that we had a convoy of around 40 ships and we were able to head back.

Here's some good news. . . .I've been promoted to first class. I'm able to double the amount of money I can send home. I hope we can get a place of our own soon.

Delbert

Dallas County, Iowa
January 1943

Late one night, the phone rang in the Wilson home, long-short-long.

"I wonder who that could be!" Leora got up from mending overalls to answer.

"Mom, it's me! Delbert! I'm at the depot in Adel. Can someone come and get me?"

"Oh, of course, son!" Leora laughed with excitement. "We'll be right there. Probably one of your brothers."

Danny offered and Junior wanted to go along as well. They grabbed their coats, warmed up the Plymouth, and drove the ten miles to Adel. Delbert piled into the car with his big bag, greeting his younger brothers.

"We thought you couldn't get a furlough."

"I thought so, too, but the engineering department had a change of heart. I'm so glad to get home and surprise everyone."

When they arrived at the farmhouse, smoke drifted from the chimney, Spats greeted them in the driveway, and the aroma of coffee welcomed Delbert home. After lots of pats on the back, the family sat at the kitchen table lit with a mantle lamp, with cups of coffee. The fragrance of Clabe's pipe was also a comfort as they sat back to listen to Delbert's stories.

"It's so good to have you home." Leora parked the coffeepot on the iron kitchen stove. "We waited and waited for a letter from you. I can tell you we were all getting pretty worried."

"It was a long time not hearing from you, too!" Delbert went on to tell them more about the battles he faced during that time.

"The Nazis weren't our only enemy on this trip. We ran into a hurricane on the way back and got separated from the rest of the convoy. With our load of fuel pumped into storage in Casablanca, we were returning empty so had to ride high. Every time the wind changed, we changed our heading with the main drive engines idling. This went on for three days!"

Delbert wrapped his hands around his warm coffee and continued. "We located two destroyers from our convoy, but about four hours later, our huge mufflers caught fire. They were filled with sludge in the exhaust lines because the engines had idled so long. Those red-hot mufflers even burned off the paint in the engine room. We thought we were goners. They turned on all the vent systems and blowers so we could tolerate the engine rooms to work there.

"Flames shot from the stack fifty to seventy-five feet high! Our deck officer got a sea water fire hose, but the Captain stopped him before he got any water down to the fire and blew up the ship. Can you believe anyone could be that dumb? Anyway, the fire lit up the sky for miles. I thought that would for sure get us noticed and torpedoes from subs would hit. Everything finally died down, but we leaked oil all the way to Norfolk. Boy were we glad to get back!"

"We are so glad you are safe and home!" said Leora.

"Did you get any souvenirs?" asked Junior.

"I got a few. I picked up a handmade knife. It will be something to show my grandchildren someday."

"You gotta catch a wife, first!" Junior quipped.

"Not until the war is over."

"'Bout time to start chores." Clabe and the younger brothers began to bundle up and head out to milk the cows.

"You may as well stay upstairs like you used to." Leora cleared off the coffee cups. "I hope Doris will be home to stay a few days while you're here."

"I do, too," Delbert responded. "And I want to meet that new nephew of mine!"

"He's growing like a little pig and is just so cute," Leora told him. "When he spies Junior, he sort of bobbles his head and smiles at him. I think Spats is a little jealous of Richard. He doesn't know what to think of him."

"Well, I'll take my bag upstairs. Anything you want me to do for you while I'm home? Chop some wood? Anything?"

"I'm sure we'll think of something, Delbert. We're such a lucky family. When Donald was home, he told about when his ship was sunk at Midway."

"He *is* lucky to be alive. I wish I'd been here when he was."

"Did you know he got mail from a girlfriend while he was here?" Leora said with a slight smile.

"Do you think it's serious? Let's write him while I'm here."

They all wrote letters to Donald and Dale. Del reported that he was taking in some good chow while he was home, even cooked wheat for breakfast, which was Dale's favorite. He mentioned that Junior had grown about a foot in the last year!

Doris came home to see her oldest brother and hear his stories. Darlene and Sam came as well, along with Richard. Delbert thought he looked so cute wearing his navy cap that they took a snapshot of him. One of the days Delbert was home, he and Doris took the Plymouth over to Sam and Darlene's to ice skate on their pond.

Another day the family drove to Perry to have Delbert's picture taken at Edmondson's Studio in his uniform, just like Donald had done.

RICHARD WILSON SCAR
(WEARING DELBERT'S
CAP) WITH DARLENE.
JANUARY 1943

After Delbert left to return to his ship, an inch of hominy snow (soft hail) fell at the farm. The temperature dropped below zero. Clabe and the boys did their daily chores, plus shelled and ground corn, and took some time to ice skate on the river.

Leora kept the fire going in the cook stove, ordered one-hundred pullets and two-hundred straight-run Leghorn chicks, to be delivered in the spring.

It was business as usual on the Minburn farm.

EM 1/c Delbert G. Wilson, Perry, Iowa,
January 1943

Seattle, Washington
Early, 1943
Donald

Dear Folks,

Well, I wonder if you figured when I decided to return early from my leave the reason why. There was a pretty good reason and her name is Rose Viola Erickson of South Bend, Washington. We decided to get married.

Rose is 31, though I assure you, she doesn't look it. She knows how to take care of herself and has a good head about her. She's also a good cook. What more could a man want?

I think I was fortunate in getting a woman of middle age for the simple reason that a teenage wife would probably be trying to find out what's all out there when I'm out to sea. I know you probably saw your son married to some sweet 16-year-old and farming. Well, I did too, once. That was ten years ago.

I'm getting along the best I can, as if there was no damn war going on, always looking ahead. If those Japs get me, well...I guess they just get me. But I'll be doing my best to be a veteran of this war.

I started teaching courses for sailors who are working towards higher ratings, third and second class. I also supervise the work on the ship.

Say, does Junior really have to go into the military? I figured he'd be exempt, especially on a farm, since the deferment of farm people. Or is going into the military his own idea? Myself? I'd tell him to forget all the imagination and adventure stuff and stick to the farm there at home if at all possible. It's no picnic, but I guess it's probably hard to keep a real American out of the scrap. I was hoping Junior wouldn't have to get in this war.

Donald [age 27]

Dear Danny,

I know you are about to leave for the Army Air Corps. Don't you think that Junior should stay home where he belongs and help the folks with their work? I've already written to Junior to tell him that. You do the same and maybe we can make him see the light. I just don't see how dad will be able to farm all that ground if he doesn't have a little help. He is full of imaginations, I guess. Just like any other man his age—looking for excitement, action, and adventure.

Donald

West Coast

Delbert

Dear Mom and Dad,

I suppose you've heard the good news by now about Donald and Rose. I kinda figured he'd do it. You fellers figure out a good weddin' present and send it from all of us. I wouldn't know what to get unless it was a good gun and a cookbook. But I can't get a gun because there's no ammo available, and they wouldn't need a cookbook because Don says Rose can really cook. He had a roast beef not so long ago and said it was really good. But I guess a sunken cake or burnt toast tastes pretty good when you're in love! Judgin' from his letter, I'd say he is.

Delbert

Rose

Leora hoped her second son hadn't been trapped into marriage. She and Darlene sent them a bedspread as a wedding gift, along with some family pictures, knowing that Donald had lost all of his when the *Yorktown* was sunk.

ROSE AND DONALD WILSON, SEATTLE, WASHINGTON, JANUARY 1943

The next letter to arrive on the Minburn farm was from Rose.

Halloe Everybody!

We received the lovely bedspread and pictures. We are very happy and tickled over the spread. It's just the thing to dress the place up, too. So, thanks a million, mom!

We are sending some wedding photos and hope you like them. They aren't too bad if I do say so myself. Donald is in his uniform and I have a dark dress with a heart shaped necklace.

I was telling Don last night that I thought I was going to like my new mother-in-law. He just grinned and told me we would get along swell. I like the way you write—such nice, long, and friendly letters. It sure makes me feel more at home, too, as I never knew my own mother. She died when I was two years old.

Gee, if I was back there, I just know we would have roast goose for dinner. I don't think I could resist taking a shot at one! I used to hunt ducks and trap stuff like that.

Thanks again for the gift. I'll be sure to write often.

Rose

Jefferson Barracks, Missouri
February 1943
Danny

Danny Wilson was anxious to get going into the Air Corps. Before he left Minburn, Sam and Darlene drove over and Sam took a picture with a box camera of the somber family lined up in their driveway. Junior wore a zipped leather jacket; Clabe had on a long coat, wore glasses and a hat; Darlene had her hands in her coat pockets; Delbert—still home on leave—wore his uniform, pea coat, tilted cap, and held a pipe; and Leora was bundled up in her new blue coat and jaunty-feathered hat that Doris helped her pick out.

DANNY LEAVING FOR THE AAF. JUNIOR, CLABE, DARLENE, DELBERT, DANNY, LEORA. JANUARY 31, 1943

Dale advised Danny that the cadets would joke around with him at first. Things would be confusing, but to remember that everyone is just like him and had been in his shoes just four weeks earlier. He told Danny that even if the other cadets seem strange, they, too, are crazy about airplanes, and they think about home, the war, and keeping from washing out, just like Danny would be thinking. "Just work hard and do your best!" Dale told him.

Dale had taken for granted that Danny would start his training on the west coast like he did. But Danny was sent to Jefferson Barracks, Missouri, fifteen miles south of St. Louis along the Mississippi River.

The first letter from home he received was from Doris.

Dear Danny,

I think this is the first letter I've ever written to you! I'll do my best so it won't be the last one! Ha! I just want you to know that whether you turn out to be a grease monkey or an ace, you'll still be a swell brother to me!

Doris

Dear Mom and Dad,

They are keeping us busy marching, hauling wood, keeping the fires on the street going, doing calisthenics, and pulling guard duty. I had to ask permission to mail a letter.

I found out how swell receiving a letter from one of the gang is. Mail call is the most important thing of the day and chow call is next!

Junior—if some of these guys here can get into the Air Corps, then you should have no problem getting in. The main thing is to be in good physical condition.

For preflight training, we all get scattered to colleges and universities around the Midwest. I'm hoping to be sent north to good old Iowa!

I saw Griff Williams and his orchestra over at the tent area last Sunday. It was free and he has a pretty good orchestra. I went over with some buddies from this hut.

Six P-38s went over in formation this afternoon. They were the excitement of the day.

Danny

Danny had not taken Don's advice about talking Junior into staying home and helping out on the farm.

Roswell, New Mexico
Early 1943
Dale

Dear Mom and Dad,

Boy-oh-boy, my wings are within sight! Only two months to go before I get my commission as a Second Lieutenant. Of course, first I have to learn to fly these twin-engine planes without having an accident or some tough luck.

Flying twin-engine planes isn't as bad as I thought it would be. Before I go overseas, I could be sent to light, medium or heavy bombardment. That will determine the plane I'll eventually fly in combat.

Junior, if I were you, I'd stay and help there on the farm for a while yet. The longer you stay out, the longer it will be before you get into the mess. The war is just beginning for the United States and I'm going to see plenty of action, no doubt. The war in the air is a bloody one. It's going to cost a lot of planes and pilots to smash our enemies.

I love getting letters from home, and so do the others in the barracks! They all enjoy hearing from you, Mom and Dad, as well as Danny and Junior.

Dale

Dale

Graduation

Dale sent home a graduation announcement and a letter.

Roswell Army Flying School's Class 43-B graduation was held Saturday, February 6, 1943 at 9:00 a.m. in the Post Theater.

Dear Mom and Dad,

I'm now Second Lieutenant, Air Corps in the United States Army and have my silver pilot's wings.

All of us new Lieutenants smoked cigars after the ceremony. I spent the rest of the afternoon in my tent—sick!

Dale

Doris

Dear Dale,

We are so proud of you! If you had washed out or even just been a grease monkey, we would have been just as proud. But you made it! Just what you wanted to be all your life! Congratulations!

Doris

Dallas County, Iowa
Early 1943
Dale

After a lot of standing and waiting in line with a big suitcase and two canvas bags, Dale got a train ticket to Des Moines, then caught a bus to Panther Corner near Minburn. Someone there noticed his uniform.

"Are you a brother of Doris Wilson?"

"Sure am." Dale was loaded with his bags.

"You want a ride to the farm?" the stranger asked.

"That'd be great! Thanks."

The two drove out to the family's home where Spats greeted them and alerted the family of a car coming up the driveway. They had been waiting for a phone call, but here was Dale, already home.

"Dale, boy! It's grand to have you home," greeted Leora. "Does your friend want to come in?"

"No. He knows Doris and just gave me a ride. It's so good to be home." Spats kept circling him and sniffing his shoes.

"You look so good in your uniform! Look at those wings!"

"They were worth it, Mom. I've got some you can wear on your coat. New pilots get an extra pair to give to their mom or wife."

"How nice. Why don't you go get changed? The others will be in soon."

Dale took his bags upstairs and changed into his familiar overalls. By the time he came back down, Spats recognized him as his old pal, wagging his tail and wanting to be patted.

"When can I meet my new nephew?" Dale asked.

"We'll plan to go this afternoon. Maybe Darlene and little Richard can come home with us for a few days."

That is just what they did. Doris was also able to come home, staying in the extra bedroom downstairs with Darlene and baby Richard. When Sam came over, some of them ice skated on the bayou across the road, just east of the house. One day everyone but Clabe went into town to watch a Jack Benny movie, *George Washington Slept Here.*

While he was home, Dale wrote a letter to Danny.

Dear Danny,

It sure seems good to be home again. I wish you were still home, but that's just how it goes.

We've been busy here catching up, skating, and playing with baby Richard.

I'll be flying a B-25 in Transition Training. It isn't what I wanted, but I already logged 25 hours in the B-25 when I was at Roswell.

Dale

When Danny noticed Dale's handwriting on the envelope, he knew that Dale had been home:

Dear Dale,

Boy, I'll bet the talk at home has changed from the Navy to the Air Corps! I sure wish I could see you. I will have to salute you now when I do. And I would do it quite proudly.

Danny

Dale's furlough was over too soon. It was his turn to have his picture taken in Perry at Edmonson's Studio. He was broad-shouldered and confident wearing his silver lieutenant bars and cherished wings of an army pilot on his dark uniform.

LT. DALE R. WILSON, PERRY, IOWA, FEBRUARY 1943

On the way back to the train station in Des Moines, Dale stopped at the Johnston High School so he could say "hello" to W.D. Clampitt, who had been their superintendent at Dexter High School. Mr. Clampitt introduced Dale to his senior class and asked him to say a few words. Afterwards, Mr. Clampitt walked out to the car to greet Clabe and Leora and ask about the others.

Before leaving Des Moines, they picked up Doris from Bishop's Cafeteria. In uniform, Dale wowed the other waitresses, and on the street, WAACs saluted him since he was now an officer.

It was the only time his parents saw one of their boys return a salute.

As the train began to pull out of the station, steam gushed up and almost kept them from waving good-bye.

"My, I hope Dale gets to come home again before he goes overseas." Leora waved with a gloved hand.

"We all do," agreed Doris.

CHAPTER 6

Spring 1943

East Coast to Aruba
Spring, 1943
Delbert

The next letter to arrive home from Delbert was a like a diary series. The entries were terse which was unusual for Delbert. Back on the tanker *Maumee*, the letter began in February and ended over a month later in March.

Feb. 10th—*We have been cruising around in the bay today, testing our new gear. Can't say what it is, but it will fool a Nazi sub commander and his torpedoes. We are headed for New York now and then off to the great unknown.*

Feb. 15th—*A flock of oil tankers with the Maumee in the lead are now nearing the coast of Florida. Yes, we saw New York, but only for about three hours. Just long enough to take on some oil. The convoy left ahead of us so as soon as we got the oil on board, we swung around and shot out of New York harbor at full speed—13 knots. We caught the convoy late that day. The fellows sure were disappointed at not being able to make a liberty in New York. I reminded everyone that we are, in fact, at war.*

We are out of the snow and zero weather. The sun is shining here and it's very warm. Most of the tankers are empty so I guess we are headed for some place to land. Aruba, an island off the coast of Venezuela, is a great oil center as the Nazi subs shelled the place a while back.

Feb. 20th—*We are down below Cuba now. We didn't stop, just drove by slowly. It's getting warmer every day. We have been sun bathing for the past two days. I have a sunburn, along with most of the crew. Sure is a change from New York's snow and zero weather. We will freeze if we go back there.*

Haven't run into any trouble here so far. We are well escorted, and this area is well patrolled by Douglas B-23s and Martin PMB-3s.

Had an emergency General Quarters/battle stations the other night. Everyone made their stations on the triple. It was just a sailboat that went by right down the middle of the convoy. We didn't even stop to investigate him.

Feb. 21st—Typical Panamanian weather today. It's hot, sultry and frequent rain squalls. Our convoy is slowly making its listless way somewhere in the Caribbean Sea. We are going southeast now, so I'm pretty sure we are headed for Aruba.

The Captain did an inspection of personnel this morning. This, no doubt, is the only tanker in the whole damn fleet that does. Reckon he wants to know if everybody has a white uniform.

Feb. 23rd—We are now in Aruba, Dutch West Indies. Did not contact but one sub on the way down, about 200 miles from here. A patrol bomber dropped depth charges. I didn't hear if they got him. The ol' Maumee is getting her belly full of oil and fuel again. Aruba is some fueling station, all right. Convoy after convoy of tankers and supply ships come and go. The sub commanders make it a point to get 'em loaded. They got one this afternoon. I could see black smoke on the horizon about 75 miles out. The survivors were landed here. Never heard how many didn't make it.

Feb. 24th—We are leaving Aruba today. The fellows aren't betting, but they are talking of our chances of getting to port with this load. Don't know where we are going yet. Most of us are confident about getting through as we are better armed than ever before. The gun crews tested everything on the way down. Not a bad rifle we have. It sure does crack. They are testing the main engines now, so it won't be long before we move out of here.

Feb. 28th—We are hammering along at 8 knots somewhere in the vicinity of Cuba. Still no subs. The weather is perfect. I'm getting a good tan. Nothing much happened today except when the lookouts spotted some nurses on a ship next to ours. Helped break the monotony of looking for periscopes. The O.D. (Officer of the Day) made them quit, however.

Mar. 7th—*We are headed for New York for sure, as we have passed up Norfolk. Everyone is glad of it even if they are about to freeze. It's freezing, all right. There is ice all over the main deck. We are due to get in about a day after tomorrow.*

Mar. 10th—*I haven't heard from Don yet. It kinda surprised me him getting hitched up to a gal like that. But it's probably the best thing for him. No doubt she will make a better home for him and happier than some kid. Men can stand this war a lot better if they have somebody like a trusting wife, or even a real gal friend.*

Well, best of luck to you all. Keep looking for places.

Delbert

Greenville, South Carolina
Spring 1943
Dale

Dale was sent to South Carolina for Transition Training. He began to type his letters.

Dear Folks,

The Greenville Army Air Base is one of the nicest places I've been stationed so far. There's plenty of grass, trees, and rain. It's a lot different from the dry, barren southwest. But the southwest had some good flying weather. I guess that's why most of the training schools are located there.

Most of this country is hills and timber, which makes it, shall we say, embarrassing to "grease" in one of the 26,000 pounds of airplane in a forced landing. It would be a little rough to land on, and one of these planes glides like a rock in case of complete power failure. It's difficult to establish a graveyard glide as we often did in Primary. Now I wonder how the Stearman could be stalled. Ha!

I sure missed getting to see Danny and Delbert when I was home. I hope I get to see them before I am sent into combat. I want to see some action in this war, though.

I wish I could fly home from Greenville now and help with the spring planting. I know it will soon be time to sow oats and start tearing up the soil again. I don't think I would want to farm all the time, but I may change my mind after combat. The farm is a darn good place to be now and after the war.

Has Doris made up her mind about joining the WAVES? I think Junior and Doris should help you there at home. At least for this summer.

Donald also thinks Junior should stay with you folks. We all know he is just as big and tough as anyone, but he should still stay where he belongs.

The Air Corps is using more B-25s in combat now, taking out the lower turret and installing waist guns for low altitude strafing and bombing. The newest ones have 1950 horsepower engines. I hoped they would be quite a bit faster. I'd still rather fly a fighter plane, but it's all about what the Army needs, not what the pilot wants. It would be swell if I had Danny as a copilot someday. All of us here in Greenville wanted to be pilots, but some are being made copilots for missing Ground School or by flipping a coin. The B-25 is not the plane I wanted to go into combat with, but for bombers, it is one of the best.

I do wish I could transfer into something else like a P-38. There I would be alone, having my own plane and guns, and responsible for my own life, as far as the airplane goes. At least I wouldn't have to sit there and have five other men in the plane and not be controlling any guns myself.

We had a visit from General H.H. "Hap" Arnold. He told us we were some of the best in the world with some of the best equipment. The sooner we get into combat, the sooner we could get back to normal is what he said. We learned that we would be fighting the most brutal, treacherous, and merciless enemy. There will be a lot of hard, bloody fighting ahead of us. There's bound to be some disappointments and setbacks. We'll have to be tougher and more brutal than the enemy.

On a happier note, a buddy of mine from Newton, North Carolina invited me to his home for some fried chicken. It's some pretty swell hospitality down here with a lot of "yo-all" talk.

I heard you folks looked at another acreage to buy. Does it have a place to land a B-25 on? Ha!

Dale

Leora

Dear Dale,

It's been just a year ago since you entered the Army Air Corps. We are going to come through this mess okay, Dale. We have a pretty lucky family and I have a feeling it is going to continue. You be careful and don't take any chances.

Mom

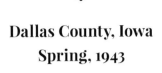

Dallas County, Iowa
Spring, 1943
Junior

Dear Danny,

I could enlist in Naval flying since I'm 17, but in the Army, they'd put me on inactive reserve until I turn 18. The Army has better planes, though. Well, whatever it is, it's going to be flying, by golly. If I can pass the screening test. I have an Aviation Mathematics book that I'm studying.

I'll have to teach dad to run the tractor and the car. I guess Uncle Sam is going to have all of us. Doris is joining the WAVES. The winders here are plastered with service flags and the house is full of pictures. We got a big picture of an A-20A hung up, too.

Dale says he's pretty good down there in South Carolina. Says he likes the B-25 better than the B-26. They have 75 mm cannons in the nose of some of the B-25s. Says it slows the plane down 18 mph every time it fires. Remember when we said they would come to this? Some other guy must have had the same idea.

Eight or nine B-17Es went over this morning, three of them in formation. They were lower than the dickens. The noise even rippled the water in the river.

There is too much farming for just dad and I. Too damn many sows and too much of the famous Iowa soil. We're doing our best, though. The landlord thinks all there is to farming is to have a lot of land, a mess of sows, and a tractor. Then he can just haul in the money! Oh yes, I left out the two farm hands. Dad and I are in that category.

That's about all I can squeeze out of this pen. Until next time, so long, good luck and study hard.

Your Brother,
C.J. Wilson

Leora

Dear Dale,

March means mud around here, and mud makes all of our chores a lot more work. There's really too much farm work for your dad and Junior. They also had to clean out and haul the feeding troughs so they are ready for farrowing sows with new babies. There's always muddy boots to scrape outside the back door, muddy overalls to put through the washing machine, and a muddy path to the clothesline. But daylight is longer and the weather is warmer. The meadowlark song has returned to these Iowa fields.

Junior drove me to town to pick up the 300 chicks I ordered. They are doing fine and the brooder stove is working so nice. I don't get up in the night to look at it, and not much during the day either.

We are having a new well dug next to the house, near the white rose bush and close to the back door. We will be able to attach a pipe or hose and pump it in the basement window for baths this summer. Whee—running water! It will be so much handier than carrying water uphill to the house.

A B-25 flew over the farm last week. Junior can name them all. He should be able to—he studies those airplane magazines and gets new ones every so often, just like you and Danny did. Sometimes when Junior and your dad are out working, they hear a plane and Junior goes to see what kind, or listens if he can't see it, and names what it is. Dad laughs and says 'Well, we must get busy when Junior names that plane.' Ha.

Mom

Dallas County, Iowa
March, 1943
Doris

"Mom!" Doris hollered at the back door. "I'm getting married!" Junior had just picked her up at the train station in Minburn. "Instead of joining the WAVES I'm joining the wives!"

"Why Doris, that's wonderful! How soon? Come talk with me in the basement. I'm just getting ready to do the wash."

"It depends on when Warren can get a furlough. Let me get changed and I'll be down to help."

Doris lugged her suitcases into the extra room, changed into a housedress, and carried her own laundry down to the basement.

"What good news, Doris. How did you decide so quickly?" Leora asked.

"Well, when Warren heard that I planned to join the WAVES and be sent off somewhere, he said he was afraid we'd never get together, so did I want to marry him now? I said 'yes!'"

Warren Neal was an Iowa farmer who had received his wings the same day Dale got his. A few days after Warren graduated at Marfa Army Air Base, he began teaching advanced students.

"If he can get a furlough after this class graduates in May, the wedding will be here. Otherwise, I'll just take the train and we'll get married in Texas." She gave her mother a hug and sorted her own clothes, adding most of them to the first batch of light-colored clothing.

"That sure leaves things up in the air, doesn't it?" Leora said.

"You know, any more it seems like everything is up in the air. Are those ready to go in the wash?"

"I guess you're right. Here's the first load. Warren is a good man. He will make a fine husband. Did you know that Richard sits alone now?"

"Oh, that cute little codger! I hope to see them again soon. Any teeth yet?"

"Yes, the first one. Sam said he was so glad it showed up because Darlene and I had looked for it for so long! Did Delbert tell you that he made a transfer?"

After the clothes had agitated for a few minutes, Doris used a wooden spoon to feed each piece through a double wringer and into a tub of hot rinse water.

"No, what's he doing now?"

"After his ship pulled into Philadelphia, he checked some notices and found they needed someone with his rating for another ship, so he put in for it." A wispy net kept Leora's hair out of her eyes, but perspiration began to trickle down her face from the humidity in the basement. "He figured anything would be safer than an oil tanker. His old ship headed to North Africa again."

"I'm so glad. Waiting for a letter from him over Christmas was nerve wracking. What kind of ship is he on now?" Doris began feeding the clothes from the hot rinse through the wringer and into a tub of cool water.

"Something new, I think. In Baltimore. The sailors can't even stay on it yet. The Navy has put them up in a nice hotel there. Say, Doris, why don't you get this first load out on the line while I start the next one."

With a wicker clothes basket on her hip, Doris hauled a load of wash up the stairs and out the back door to peg things on the clothesline. The spring timber bloomed white with fragrant Juneberries.

Baltimore, Maryland
March 1943
Delbert

Dear Folks,

I met a really nice girl who is in the Coast Guard. Her job was to check us all in and out while working on the ship. She doesn't smoke or drink and seems quite sensible. She's different from a lot of other girls. Either that or she's a really good actress. Ha!

Tell Darlene that I heard that fathers have a separate rating, so Sam probably won't be drafted. He is doing a hell of a lot more good where he is at.

And so are you, Junior. I wish I could make you realize it. I know you want to fly, so do I, but there is plenty of time for that. We will have two experts in the family to teach us after the war. I'd wait a while, yet. Maybe you can time it so you will be in basic or advanced when the war is over. No use stickin' yer neck out 'till you have to. To hell with so-called glory, medals, and heroism. It's the guys who stay around close and healthy that will enjoy the confetti, if any, after this damn war. Not the men with bruised brains of battle. Modern war is hard enough for men to realize, who have seen some of it. I figure it's something to stay away from as long as you can. You don't need any part of it yet, Junior.

Delbert

When Delbert's new ship, the USS *Achelous*, sailed with a convoy bound for North Africa, Delbert wasn't aboard. He'd come down with the mumps.

Dallas County, Iowa
May 1943
Leora

May was a busy month. Doris bought an aqua suit as her wedding outfit for $25.45 at Taylor's Seventh and Walnut, "Where Des Moines Shops with Confidence." She also bought white, ankle-strap, peep-toe shoes from Baker's on Seventh for $5.61.

Leora received Mother's Day cards from all four sons in the service. Darlene and her family came for the day, which was her first Mother's Day. Richard kept them all entertained.

Dale had sent Leora a satin pillow-top, with a B-25 on it.

Warren was given three days off. He couldn't miss the start of his next class of advanced cadets, so the wedding date still depended on what day he could fly back to Iowa. He was able to catch a ride home on a Saturday in May and they were married the next afternoon. On May 16, 1943, Doris Wilson became Mrs. Warren Neal in Dexter, Iowa, at the Presbyterian church where Warren's family attended services.

Leora wrote to everyone about the wedding, that Doris wore her new aqua suit, white shoes and hat, and carried a little white Bible. She and Darlene wore pink roses and white gardenias. Warren, of course, was in his Lieutenant's uniform with his wings. Darlene was the matron of honor and, since Warren's brother Willis was also in the Air Corps, Warren's brother-in-law Mervin Wells was the best man. Warren's sister, Nadine played the pump organ and sister Betty Neal Wells sang a solo. For the recessional, Nadine played the Air Force Song, "Off we go, into the wild blue yonder."

LT. WARREN AND DORIS NEAL, DEXTER PRESBY-
TERIAN CHURCH, MAY 1943

Norfolk, Virginia
May 1943
Delbert

After twenty-four days with the mumps, Delbert was finally out of the hospital. He sent Doris $100 as a wedding present. Then he sent telegrams home three days in a row:

NORFOLK, VIRGINIA, MAY 19, 1943. GOOD NEWS GOT SCHOOL STARTING SOON GOING TO BALTIMORE FOR A FEW DAYS LOVE DEL

BALTIMORE, MD, MAY 20, 1943. WIRE $150. MAY GET MARRIED HAVING A WONDERFUL TIME LOVE DEL

BALTIMORE, MD. MAY 21, 1943. GETTING MARRIED SUNDAY MAY 23 TO MISS EVELYN MOORE. LOVE TO YOU ALL DEL

Dallas County, Iowa
May 1943

Leora

Leora started using carbon paper so she could make duplicates of news she would write to everyone.

EVELYN AND DELBERT WILSON, JUNE 1943, NORFOLK, VIRGINIA

So much has happened in a few days that I hardly know where to begin. Doris and Warren left for Marfa, Texas on the 20th. Just after dinner that same day we got a phone call that we had a Western Union telegram at the depot—it was from Delbert. He said he was to be married Sunday, May 23rd to Evelyn Moore of Baltimore! Some surprise now, isn't it?!

On Sunday evening we got a long-distance call from Baltimore. It was Delbert and Evelyn! We had a good talk. Darlene and Richard were here. Darlene, Dad and I talked to Delbert, and Darlene and I talked to Evelyn. She said she was so happy and was anxious to meet all of us. Delbert said he was happy. He asked about the farming, the Plymouth and you boys.

Dale

All I can say is that Evelyn Moore is pretty darn lucky. She must be a swell girl. There isn't a better guy than Del anywhere.

Dale

CHAPTER 7

Summer 1943

Dallas County, Iowa
Summer, 1943
Donald

Donald Wilson was selected for Electrical Interior Communications school in Washington, DC. He and Rose decided to take a train across the country from Seattle and stop in Iowa so Rose could meet her in-laws. She would stay on the farm until Donald found them a place to live. "Don't go to any unnecessary preparations. The Mrs. is just common people too," Donald wrote home ahead of time. "I figured she could just as well visit and take in the Midwest climate and food for a while 'till I get into Naval Housing. She's trying to tell me she's scared, but she's having the time of her life, I believe."

Donald also told Junior to have a little bait ready for fishing.

Leora's mother, Grandmother Goff, also wrote and said that she and Leora's brother Willis would be visiting. Unfortunately, they missed seeing Donald by two days but got to meet Rose.

"I'm so glad to get to know all of you," Rose told them. "There's only men left in my family at home, so this is really special for me."

"We're glad you could stay extra days," Leora told her, "and that Darlene and Richard could stay longer, too. Let's get more pictures taken while you are here."

"Good idea. I'll get my Kodak." Rose snuffed out a cigarette. One snapshot was of Grandmother sitting in a rocking chair in the yard, with Rose perched on the arm. And one of Rose and Darlene sitting in the grass with their arms around each other.

"I smell a skunk," Leora said.

"I do too." Darlene stood, looking toward the west. "That might be what's wandering around over on the side hill. Isn't it acting strange?"

"Where? I've never seen one." Rose joined Darlene. "Is it dangerous or just a nuisance?"

"Well, wandering around in the daytime like this, it could have rabies."

"I reckon I could shoot it for you, if you like."

Rose certainly was an outdoor girl who enjoyed fishing, hiking, and hunting. Donald had said he kind of hated to hunt with her because she was so much competition. Rose hit the skunk with her second shot.

As soon as Donald found housing for them, Rose started out for Washington, D.C.

Leora

Dear Dale,

Rose was so easy to get acquainted with. She's a good worker. It seemed like we have known her for a long time. If she didn't smoke, I think she would be about perfect.

Your dad helped me pick strawberries after everyone left. I remember that used to be your job!

I had to put the chickens in the corn crib. An owl has been chasing them. I'll have to make a scarecrow to keep the owls away.

Delbert is out on the East Coast going to school. He and Donald were able to get together over a weekend and they met each other's wives.

Junior just devoured a big dishpan full of mixed lettuce, spinach, kale, endive, and parsley. He reminds us often that we need to stay healthy.

Uncle Clarence Goff thinks this war will be over by Christmas. How wonderful that would be. I do hope it will come true.

I sold twenty-five Grade-A Leghorn roosters, and my chickens lay over six or seven dozen eggs every day! Plenty to eat and sell. I also make and sell butter.

I'm doing what I can so we can have a place of our own soon. A place for all of you to come home to after this war.

Love,
Mom

LEORA, "JUST COMING FROM FEEDING THE CHICKS
AND GATHERING THE EGGS." JUNE 1943

Marfa, Texas
Summer, 1943
Doris

Doris and Warren rode to Marfa, Texas, with another couple. Places to rent were scarce, and at first they lived in the Crews Hotel. Doris asked her mother to pack the rest of her stuff in an old suitcase and ship it down. "Be sure to send news about Del and the rest of the boys," she added.

Dear Mom and Dad,

I just went to an officers' wives tea at Mrs. Hoyle's. It wasn't as bad as I thought it might be. Practically everyone knew what the score was but me and I wonder sometimes if I shall ever catch on to Army life and lingo. Mom, you would be surprised how really complicated it is. We don't call each other by our first names, but rather "Mrs. Such-and-Such."

It's hard to get appliances here. I might have to send money home for you to buy things that I cannot get in Marfa. A coffee maker, toaster, and hot plate would be quite handy.

Have you heard from Dale recently? I'd like to know how much longer he will be in school. When I read your letter about Dale's recent trips, I had a dream about him flying here and Warren introduced him to all the Majors and Colonels on the place. Gee, I was proud! They liked him too, in my dream. It sure would be great if he could come over this way.

Well, we can sort of relax with our four boys in school, can't we? Wish this mess would clear up before any of them get out and before some crazy student wrecks a plane with my husband in it. But everyone down here plans for five more years of it.

Warren and I went to a graduation of one of his cadets where we saw actress Ann Sothern and her husband, actor Robert Sterling. Sterling was a cadet. They are just people, too. I was disappointed. Ha! There were lots of flash bulbs popping, though.

Write again soon. A letter a day wouldn't be too often. I can't wait to see little Richard again.

Love to all,
Doris

Dear Dale,

I've seen a B-17! It went over Marfa and I could tell it wasn't an AT-17. I'll bet you are laughing right now to read this!

I think Mom is in the height of her glory with all this marrying business going on. I can just hear her gabbin' over the phone about everything. She sure gets a kick out of things.

Well, take a lot of hot sun here in Texas, along with hot sand, dust, sagebrush, a few mountains, tall, lean men with western hats, tight pants, and high-heeled boots. There are a lot of Mexicans here as well. There you have it...all from the eyes of an outsider from Iowa! Texans take their heritage quite seriously. To them, they don't live in the U.S. A Texan lives in Texas, and he is proud of it.

As for me, give me God's country. People who have never lived in Iowa have really missed something, if only the change of seasons. That's enough, right there.

Doris

To Warren's folks, Kenneth and Ruby Neal, Dexter, Iowa

Dear Mr. and Mrs. Neal,

I like Texas pretty well, but its main asset to me is an absolutely wonderful husband. Texas is Okay for the Texans. But if they want to be satisfied with it, they better not visit Iowa. Ha! I do get a kick out of the little kids who'd like to be friendly but are too bashful. And Warren when he lets loose of my hand, taking his cigarette from his mouth so he can salute back at some eager Air Cadet—yes, I get a kick out of that too. I'm really having a wonderful time here.

Doris

The Iowa waitress turned officer's wife had never had a formal gown but needed one for the opening of Marfa's new Officer's Club. She rode with another pilot's wife to Alpine to get dresses. Doris chose an aqua one, about the same color as her wedding suit. It was short-sleeved, accented by lots of small ruffles. The other young woman loaned her a pearl necklace and bracelet.

Doris wrote home that she felt like Cinderella at the dance and had fun.

Orders for Combat
Summer, 1943

Dale

Dale finished Transition at Greenville and was put on a combat crew as a "damn copilot," as was the rest of his class.

Dear Mom and Dad,

Lieutenant J.M. Wieland graduated in an earlier class and he is my pilot. He let me fly the plane half the time and gave me all the instrument time I need since he already had plenty. All of us copilots in the B-25 are bombardiers. When we practiced skip bombing, I dropped eight bombs and scored three bulls-eyes while approaching the target about 25 feet above the trees, then letting down on our target. It is a real sport. We were traveling 230 MPH and that seems fairly fast when we are clipping the treetops.

I saw the Atlantic Ocean for the first time when we flew the planes to the coast to fire the guns. When I fired the 75-millimeter, flames flashed out in front of us and it seemed to almost stop the plane for a fraction of a second.

We flew to the Bahamas, taking off at 0500 and returning at 1300— eight continuous hours in the air! It was a round-robin of 1600 miles. 1100 miles of it was over water.

The 70-mm packs a wallop. I fired three rounds and scored two hits out of three. Each round costs a war bond of $18.75.

It's possible that we may have to fly several different planes in combat, including fighters. In some theaters, the copilots got to fly P-38s. I like the sound of that.

145

I hope to get home again before leaving for combat and have some real food. Some of that good lettuce, spinach, and whole wheat with plenty of milk and eggs sounds pretty good right now.

I'll keep writing.

Dale

Dallas County, Iowa
Summer, 1943

Junior

Dear Dale,

Two P-47 Thunderbolts went over the other day. Pretty darn good plane. Lots of noise, speed, good design which are essential. I wouldn't mind being in one now.

I guess I'm going to be a farmer for the duration. I wrote to Des Moines for an application for the Army Air Corps. The application came back with a slip of paper that said: "I hereby certify that I am not an agricultural worker, that my parents do not live on a farm, and are not in any way connected with the agricultural industry." There was other red tape with it and the seal and sign of a Notary Public to go with it.

Maybe you or Dan can teach me to fly a "Cub." Ha! I'll never lose interest in flying, though.

I finally got the plowing done and the corn is planted and up. We are just as far ahead as the rest of the farmers. Got the John Deere all dressed up in its summer costume—the cultivator. The tractor really has had a workout this spring, but it keeps puttin' right along with that familiar chug.

Getting lots of raw spinach, lettuce, kale, endive, and other greens to eat. I'm taking good care of my health. All the trees are fully leafed, everything is green as the devil and I feel fine. I hope you do, too.

Keep 'em flying and I'll keep farming. Wish you an abundance of luck and admiration.

Junior

Preparing for Combat
Summer, 1943
Dale

Dear Mom and Dad,

Can you send an olive drab uniform to me? And ask Junior if he doesn't want that big skinning hunting knife, I'd like to have it. I have a new .45 automatic, but that knife would come in handy, too. Then I'll be all set. Except for flying a P-38. Ha!

I still don't like the bombers because there are too many men in one plane. I want something that can be turned upside down, something maneuverable.

Our crew left Greenville by rail on July 3rd. We headed for Savannah, Georgia, and drew our overseas equipment and a new B-25G. We flew over Roswell, New Mexico, and Gardner Field at Taft, California. When I got over Gardner, I realized how close I was to Danny. It made me feel a little sick. It is impossible to see him now. We are allowed to write home and phone. I think I'll call Danny and see if I can talk with him a while.

We also flew over Boulder Dam, the Grand Canyon, the Golden Gate Bridge, and Mare Island Navy Yard with its balloon barrage. We processed for overseas in the Sacramento area while the plane was made ready for its long flight.

I was finally able to phone Danny here. We talked before I left the States. We could hear each other very plain. Danny thought I sounded different and I thought he did, too. Danny is doing swell and said he would be there with me. He will make it. I'm sure of that.

Dale

Dallas County, Iowa

Leora

Dear Dale,

As soon as we learned of your overseas address, I tried out my first attempt at a V-Mail letter. I can't write my usual long letters this way. They only use one side of a typing sheet and take a photo of it as a frame on a strip of film with hundreds of other letters. I suppose this is how it's done now. After it is developed, your letter will look like a four-by-five-inch letter, folded and slipped into a small envelope with your address.

You take the best care of yourself, Dale. Good luck is with all of us. We are the "Lucky Seven," you boys and girls. Be happy and keep your chin up.

Love, Mom

CLABE AND JUNIOR BY THE PUMP AT THE MINBURN FARM, JUNE 1943

Pearl Harbor
Summer, 1943
Dale

Flying overnight from Hamilton Field, San Francisco, Dale's bomber arrived in the Territory of Hawaii.

Dear Mom and Dad,

The plane's good engines purred out there on each side of us like two well-oiled sewing machines for the entire 13 hours. Our fuel consumption averaged a little over 100 gallons/hour.

Pearl Harbor still shows evidence from December 7, 1941. From the way things were chewed up, the Japs must have used almost entirely 100-pound fragmentation bombs.

We had time to visit Honolulu and see an Army and Navy baseball game. All the stores and even the bars were closed by 4:00 p.m., and everything blacked out at dusk.

Dale

The rest of Dale's letters were censored:

Dear Mom and Dad,

You have probably been looking for this letter. We have been very busy, and, in the meantime, I have requested a transfer to twin-engine fighters.

Several more pilots have put in for fighters, but all have been disapproved. Mine will no doubt be disapproved, so I guess it will be safe in giving you this address which will be my address for the long time I will be in this part of the world.

We arrived here [cut out] after spending [cut out] at the place of my last letter. That reminds me, did you get that last letter?

I cannot tell you the news like I did before. You will just have to read the newspaper for the situation in this theater of operations. We will be going north soon. I have learned quite a bit about the situation there. I think you are among the few in the U.S. that can realize this is going to be a long, tough, and rough fight.

We have done a lot of flying. This type of flying is REALLY flying. Most of the time we are buzzing. All this close formation takes skill and is a lot of work. Until we start receiving the [cut out] there will be [cut out] pilots per airplane. We split time. Lt. Wieland and I are still flying together. He will fly as pilot one mission and I will fly as pilot the next, and so on. This [cut out] is a good weapon and we'll be down where things are "hot," but surprise will help a lot I hope.

This country is old fashioned, at least the [cut out]. It looks like the U.S. around 1800-something. The town here looks like an old frontier town in the movies. This used to be one of the richest gold-mining sections and there is old excavation around the town.

Dale's transfer request was turned down. Contrary to what they'd been told at Greenville, they were all stuck with bombers. Since the Allies had decided to settle the war with Hitler first, most men and planes were being sent to Europe instead of to the Pacific Theater.

Santa Ana, California
Summer, 1943
Danny

Dear Mom and Dad,

Ever since I've been here for Preflight training, the P–38s have caught my eye. They were playing dog-tag over my head when I first arrived. They are always coming over our barracks roof in a string of four to eight. They make a whistling sound like a shell going over. Today, four P–38s dived out of the sun in a power dive. They pulled out of a dive about 500 feet up, with a roaring scream trailing after them. They went into the climb by hanging by the props for a long time, then flipped over into an Immelmann turn, one after the other. Oh boy!

We had a week of classification tests and then a physical exam. They gave me an extra hearing test because of that mastoidectomy I had when I was four. I passed.

How are things going on the farm? I suppose the corn has about all come up. The beans too, maybe. You're probably thinking of the race between button-weeds and corn on the north place. How are the pigs coming along, dad?

Down here they have thrashed and made the second crop of hay. It seems funny to me to see big fields of baled alfalfa and palm trees around the farmhouse.

And you, too, Mom. How's your chickens coming along?

Every B-25 that goes over makes me think maybe it's Dale.

Last Saturday night I went to L.A. with Dick Touet and a couple of other men. We went into the Hollywood Canteen. There was an orchestra playing and we walked right by the mike. I was surprised to see Kay Kyser walk up to the mike and then lead his orchestra. There were several movie stars there. I danced with Jane Russell at the Canteen. Can you believe it?

The chow here is very good. We've had corn on the cob a couple of times, and we had muskmelon for dinner today. This reminds me of plowing corn last year with the John Deere and stopping and uncovering the young pumpkin and melon plants. I'll admit it makes me sort of homesick.

I've been following the war news and hope the Allies would take Italy now that it was in disorder without Mussolini. It will take some time to take Germany, but it'll get done.

I suppose Junior is starting to look like a body builder now. I sure would like to grab some barbells and work out again. I keep in the best shape possible. I weigh 170 and I got the best tan in the squadron. Ha!

Have you got another shotgun, Dad? I bet you will this fall. You don't want to miss out on a little duck, pheasant, and squirrel hunting once in a while. Won't be long until the squirrels run around with walnuts. There'll be lots of fox and squirrels around after the war if you two Wilsons don't get them.

Danny

Tucson, Arizona
Summer, 1943
Danny

Danny was sent to Primary Training at Ryan Field in Tucson, Arizona, famous for cactus and sunshine. There he flew the single-wing Ryan PT-22, an open cockpit plane.

Will Touet, Dick's father who was from Osceola, Iowa, wrote to Clabe and Leora:

Dear Friends,

Will call you friends for after being with your son, Dan, at Tucson, it ought to be that way.

We spent one afternoon and evening with him and our son and was pleased to see such fine boys and the company they kept.

Sure hope the boys get to stay together and that they are successful all the way through.

We met you folks in Des Moines one time when the boys came in from Cedar Falls. Hoping for a time when we can see you again.

Will Touet

A/C Danny Wilson amd a PT-22, Ryan Field, Tucson, Arizona, October 1943

CHAPTER 8

Autumn 1943

"Next Destination"
Autumn, 1943
Dale

There were letters from Junior, Donald, Delbert, and Darlene waiting for Dale when he arrived at his "next destination." He had not heard from Danny yet.

Mom and Dad,

If I remember right, this is Richard Wilson Scar's birthday. I will always remember this day because we went on our first strike mission the same morning that Richard was born. I remember a year ago when I received the little announcement from Darlene while I was at Basic.

It is pretty humid where we are and the living conditions primitive. We found a knoll a little larger than the tent and cleared it off. We dug drainage ditches so water can run off in all directions and built a foundation for our own tent. I actually sweat more liquid than I can drink.

I hope to hear from Danny soon. He likes to write and talk about the same things that I like to write and talk about.

The skeeters here are blood-thirsty and persistent devils. Even as I type this, there is a hum of them trying to break through the net I have around me. The joke around here is "One skeeter said to the other, 'Shall we eat him here or take him outside?' and the other said 'Let's eat him here, if we go outside, the big ones will take him away!'"

I suppose by the time you receive this in Iowa, Junior will be in the Air Force. In a year or two, providing we both get bombers, all three of us ought to get on the same crew. Boy, that would be the best darn crew that ever flew in a bomber.

We are all taking Atabrine pills to prevent malaria.

How's the corn pickin' situation? I'd enjoy plowing with the John Deere again. Did Junior get the fall plowing done? It makes the farming more interesting with the tractor. Were the weeds bad in the alfalfa this year?

Do you think you will move on an acreage someplace? I think a few acres of land with a home is the nearest thing to security. When the war ends, we will have to feed the European countries and replenish their farms with livestock, machinery, seeds, etc. The demand will be great for ten or fifteen years.

How is Spats and his new pal? Does the pump by the house work all right? I believe you said something about running water. I'd like to be there and eat some of that popcorn for Christmas. And of course, fried chicken, raw carrots, and plenty of milk! And good ol' wheat for breakfast. Ha!

I have been doing some thinking, believe it or not, about what I should do when hostilities cease and I am able, if I so desire, to leave the Army. Of course, before that time there is always the possibility of two events which may directly affect my immediate, if not extended, future. But I have been thinking that they will be favorable.

I am wondering if I shouldn't go to a college and specialize in something outside of flying, like radio, for instance. At the same time, I may take up something that would improve myself towards being a better 'mixer' and conversationalist. The Army has helped me a lot, however.

On the other hand, I'm wondering if I shouldn't stay in the Air Corps or get a job in commercial flying. Yes, if I go to a school, I'll continue to fly some kind of a flying machine somewhere. I love to fly and will continue to do so as long as I am able or permitted. Sometimes I think that I would like to go to the University of Iowa, play football, and be a teacher in math, radio, or some other interesting subject. Yes, I've even thought about the possibility of getting married someday. Although the way I look at things now, this may never happen.

Of course, we can think about giving 'em hell here and winning the war as fast as we can, at present, but when we can, we all think a little about the future and just how our leaders will thrash it out without too much fighting among themselves.

Hearing "White Christmas" on the radio makes me think of Gardner Field. It is funny, but certain songs make me think of a certain place. Some songs make me homesick. I guess I'm just a sentimentalist.

I can't let you know or seem to write anything of interest that will not escape a little censoring. Wish I could.

Well, until next time. God bless you and so long. With love and wishes for the BEST of luck,

Dale

Wichita Falls, Texas
Autumn, 1943
Junior

Junior did get the okay to join the Army Air Forces. Sam and Darlene drove to Minburn to see him off. Sam, again, took the traditional picture, catching a somber family lined up in front of the Plymouth. Clabe in his leather jacket held year-old Richard, Junior in a double-breasted jacket, buttoned wrong, and holding the same suitcase his brothers had used, Darlene, and of course, Leora.

CLABE HOLDING RICHARD SCAR, JUNIOR, LEORA,
DARLENE SCAR

When Donald received the news with the photo, he kidded about Junior being so excited to leave that he shifted his jacket a button off.

Leora hung a new service flag in the farmhouse. A circle of five blue stars—one for each son in the military.

SERVICE FLAG WITH FIVE BLUE
STARS, ONE FOR EACH FAMILY
MEMBER IN THE SERVICE, MINBURN

Junior was inducted at Camp Dodge, just north of Des Moines. Leora was reminded of her three older brothers who all left from Camp Dodge to serve in the First World War.

When Junior arrived in Wichita Falls, Texas, he wrote home.

Dear Mom and Dad,

I know you had hoped I wouldn't enlist, but what would I tell my grandchildren if I stayed home on the farm?

Texas is a heck of a state. It's just reddish sand and very little ground with grass on it. We have some pretty good chow here. I just ate three big apples, three ice cream cones, and a bottle of milk! The other guys don't like the food as much because it is mostly greens, carrots, cabbage, lettuce and a little bit of fruit. All they like is cookies, cake, toast, potatoes, and meat.

There are a lot of boys in my barracks who don't smoke, and the ones who do wish they didn't when they get out for physical training. I'm glad Del got all of us boys interested in weight lifting when we were growing up. It is paying off for me now. I've gained about fifteen pounds since being here, all muscle.

Mom, when you write, can you send me copies of my "Strength & Health" magazine?

Don't you folks worry too much or work too hard. Keep busy as it covers up the lonesomeness. Have dad write once in a while if he's not too busy. Let me know what is going on at the farm—in the land of dreams! Good ol' Iowa. I'll be glad when I get to see black soil again!

Junior

It was only Clabe and Leora left on the farm. The landlord hired some men to help Clabe out from time to time. Leora kept busy writing her five sons, one daughter, and even postcards to Darlene between their visits.

Leora was used to having family around or nearby. This was the first time it was just the two of them since Delbert's birth, twenty-eight years earlier.

Stillwater, Oklahoma
Autumn, 1943

Junior

Dear Mom and Dad,

I am no longer a private! I'm officially an Aviation Student.

We had to be quarantined for a week when we arrived in Stillwater. At least until a doctor could look us all over. We are confined in our barracks now. The officer here said that Stillwater was one of the cleanest towns in the U.S. "No 'professionals'" is how he put it. I think you know what I mean.

All the boys are a clean bunch now. Since we are all prospective officer material, it's all "Mister So-and-So." No more "Soldier," or "Hey Joe." The officers call us gentlemen, not just men. We sure have to be polite and courteous. Saluting has to be just right.

Say, if you have an extra shoe stamp, can you buy me a pair of dress shoes? Plain toe, brown, size 10 ½. I like the lace type with slick leather. I think I left a $20 or two in your pocketbook, Mom. I can't dance in a pair of G.I. shoes!

I saw quite a few John Deeres on my way up from Texas. It sure made me wish I was back on it at home. How is the tractor running, Dad?

Take care and write when you can.

Junior

When the shoes his mother sent arrived, Junior reported back that they fit perfectly. He sent money home for his mother's December 4th birthday, and asked them to keep writing.

Dear Dale,

Howdy! I know how a letter is to a guy now! A letter from home is pretty swell.

I hope you are doing okay with your flying. I have your picture displayed on my shelf and all the boys ask about you. I heard Dan is in Basic now and is probably flying what you did.

Write what you can when you can. Good luck and God bless you.

With Love,
Your Brother, Junior

Tucson, Arizona
November 1943
Danny

Danny arrived at Marana Field at Tucson, thirty miles north of Ryan, for Basic Training. Instead of flying Basic Trainers at Marana, Dan was one of thirty-six cadets who went directly to Advanced Trainers.

Gold pilot's wings were embossed on the Marana Field stationary carrying Dan's confident handwriting home. He wrote detail after detail about the fighter planes instruments, gadgets, what he had to do to start, go around the pattern, and land.

⚜

Dear Mom and Dad,

I'm one of thirty-six to go straight to Advanced planes in Basic. We're sort of an experimental group. If we make it, we will go to Advanced and fly fighter planes. The time between now and January 1st will determine my fate. That word 'wash' seems to stay right on my tail.

Of the thirty-six who came from Ryan, only one buddy came with me. Len Unrath. Dick Touet went to Bakersfield, California. I sure hated to break apart from him. He really has coordination. That's what it takes to fly. Junior is coordinated and quick like Touet, so I think Junior will do okay when he gets to flying.

We run a couple miles every day, but the calisthenics is done in nice, fluffy dust. Boy would I ever like to be running up the hill by the house with good old grass. Or is it snow now? I'd run back to the timber, put my

167

hand on a jack oak, and watch a squirrel run around in the top. That will come later.

You asked me if I'd seen any ducks. Believe it or not I was with my Primary instructor and we went out one day and just hunted ducks on little ponds in the desert. He would fly just over the pond and scare them up, then come around and chase them. We'd fly right behind them. They can fly pretty fast!

One day, he was cruising around low and scared up a couple of deer. There was a guy who about went crazy when we did this because he didn't have his gun! Boy, those deer would have been duck soup from a plane. They would actually be too easy to get.

How are you doing on the farm now that all the boys are gone? How's Spats? Does he still like to go squirrel hunting?

Danny

Dear Doris,

Well, don't pass out or anything...I'm actually writing to you. Just wanted to let you know I'm still alive. I've been really busy with training. The next four weeks will decide my fate. I hope I make it okay and don't wash out. They say a guy can step from an AT-6 to a P-51 Mustang pretty well. I sat in a new P-51B with a four-bladed prop and Rolls-Royce engine. It was swell. I believe I could have flown it solo right there—on the ground! Ha!

Danny

Dallas County, Iowa
November, 1943

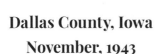

When Junior asked his mother to send one of Dale's pictures to display on a shelf, Leora wrote Dale about it, adding that Danny had done the same thing.

Dear Dale,

Oh, we are so proud of you. We think you are on the right track about what to do when this is over. You'd make a good instructor in math or any subject you like. Yes, if you find a good girl, get married and have a home.

We imagine seeing you writing letters on the typewriter in your tent. We are so glad you can hear a radio once in a while.

You are doing fine, Dale. Just keep your chin

CLABE WITH PET DOGS, SPATS AND JOE,
NOVEMBER 1943

up and do your best. This will be over sometime before long, and what a lot of experiences you'll have to tell us all.

We will write again soon. Hope you get your Christmas boxes. A prayer for you and God bless you.

Love and Good Luck Always,
Mom & Dad

CHAPTER 9

Late 1943

"Somewhere in the Southwest Pacific"
November 1943
Dale

Dale addressed his letter from "Somewhere in the Southwest Pacific" to his folks "in the good ol' U.S.A."

Dear Mom and Dad,

I received your letter of November 2nd and the Christmas package today. I was sure glad to get everything, and it will certainly come in handy. We get all the shaving cream and razor blades we need here at the P.X. but hardly ever any American candy.

I also received a letter from Doris dated November 5th. She had gotten a picture from Danny getting into a plane. I hope Dan sends me one. I have not heard from him yet.

I suppose cousin Merrill Goff has seen plenty of action. I would like to see him and give him a ride in a bomber. If you see him, say 'hello' for me and that I have been 'baptized' too.

It won't be long now before I get a crew and a plane assigned to me. Anyway, I fly half the missions as first pilot at present. I got [BLACKENED BY CENSOR] on at Greenville, S.C., as did most of my class there in that particular squadron.

I'll bet some of those days back there are swell. The timber, too. Wonderful flying weather along in the fall.

Our family is certainly doing all right for Uncle Sam. I hope we all can continue to bigger and better things.

Can you send me a flying magazine or a Reader's Digest once in a while? I know they would be appreciated by everyone.

I can say that every day is a day off the war and a day closer to victory, or that every mission is a mission off the war and a mission closer to coming home.

Dale

That is what his parents hoped for—the war to be over and their sons to be back home.

"Somewhere in New Guinea"
November 1943
Dale

Dear Mom and Dad,

I received a big letter from Darlene and a V-mail from Donald. Donald writes me pretty regular. He had gotten a picture from Dan by his Ryan. Dan said he had her up to 205…Ha! I'm sure glad he has gone on to Basic. I hope I get a picture from Dan. I haven't heard from him yet.

I now have one-fifth of my required missions. I don't know if I'll quit when I do have the required number. If I get into the latest medium bomber or the latest attack bomber, I may decide to stay over here longer. Time will tell.

Are you going to stay on the place next year? How does the John Deere run? Still have plenty of power? It will probably need new rings and sleeves pretty soon.

I suppose the farmers can still get all the fuel they need. We burn plenty of 100-octane stuff in here in order to blast these "yellow…." It's working.

It will be two Christmas days that I have been away from home. I may be home before it is three. Again, time will tell.

If you have any new pictures, I'd like to have a couple. Especially one of you both.

Love and best wishes,
Dale

Dallas County, Iowa
December 1943

Darlene

Dear Dale,

Richard is eating an apple and walking from room to room, talking. Can't quite make out what he's saying. He has 16 teeth and does pretty good but makes an apple look like a mouse after he's been after it. He's getting to be quite a big boy. Just think, he wasn't quite four months old when you last saw him. He'll be saying "Hi Dale!" by the time you see him again. We hope that won't be too long.

We love you and are rooting for you,
Darlene

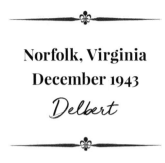

Norfolk, Virginia
December 1943

Delbert

Dear Mom and Dad,

I started the same Interior Communications School as Donald. He has only three months left. Quadratic equations are frustrating and I had only two days to learn logs. Our instructor had four months of them in college! I may be in Washington for eight months if I'm lucky. But I reckon I'll never know what it looks like. Our class started with 54 men. We are down to around 30 now. The rest are going to sea.

I had a dream about hunting pheasants with Dad, Don, Junior, Dale, and Dan. They were scouting through a cornfield and Evelyn and I were standing up on the fence and the corn was way up above—the ears about two feet long! As you fellers came through, the pheasants would get up and sail low over the corn and we would blast 'em. Sure was good shooting. I could hear dad and the boys talking and laughing as they rattled through the corn. It was the most realistic dream I have ever had.

Keep your chins up. We will all have a big reunion when the war is over.

Love,
Delbert

Evelyn

Dear Mom and Dad,

Del says he stopped over at Don's before he came home. He read your letter to Don and Rose and one from Sam. I guess little Richard has a lot of entertaining to do now as he is the only boy you all have to divide among you. I'll bet he gets enough loving for six babies! Del is crazy about babies.

We are expecting a baby in June. Are you surprised? I just couldn't keep it a secret any longer! I guess I don't have to tell you how thrilled we are.

Love,
Evelyn

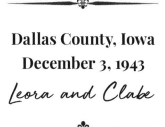

Dallas County, Iowa
December 3, 1943
Leora and Clabe

A western Union telegram was delivered on Leora's fifty-third birthday. It was written in pencil.

> *WUX Washington DC*
> *654 PM*
> *Dec 3, 1943*
> *To Clabe D Wilson*
> *Rte. No 1*
> *Minburn, Iowa*

The secretary of war desires me to express his regret that your son, second Lieutenant Dale R. Wilson, has been reported missing in action since twenty-seven November over New Guinea. If further details or other information are received, you will be promptly notified.

Uliotz Adjutant General

A few days later, a letter from Dale's commanding officer was in their mailbox.

My Dear Mrs. Wilson,

One of the saddest duties that I have been called on to perform during my Army service is to notify you that your son, Second Lieutenant DALE

R. WILSON, has been missing in action since November 27, 1943. The aircraft in which he was Co-pilot was engaged by the enemy and forced down over enemy territory somewhere in the Southwest Pacific Area after having accomplished its Mission in an excellent manner.

It was not my good fortune to have known Dale intimately very long, but in the five months that he served with me, he grew each day in the respect and admiration of the entire Command. His zeal in action, his extraordinary professional knowledge, and the honesty of his character endeared him to all with whom he came in contact.

The entire Command joins me in expressing to you our sincere and heartfelt sorrow. You may rest assured that the great work that he started will be continued and his name will live long within his organization.

You, no doubt, will desire Dale's effects. These have been inventoried and will be retained here for a period of ninety days, after which they will be sent to the Effects Quartermaster, Kansas City Quartermaster Depot, Kansas City, Missouri, for forwarding to you. For further information regarding his effects, you are advised to communicate directly with the Effects Quartermaster.

You may be infinitely proud of your son, as we all are. The example of courage, friendliness, and good sportsmanship which he set will always serve as a beacon to us, and we are anxiously awaiting his possible return. If there is anything that I can do for you, please do not hesitate to call on me.

Holland Legg, Major, Air Corps, Commanding Officer

Darlene drove over to her folks' as soon as she heard. She and her mother called family members who had phones and wrote all the rest with the bad news.

Evelyn answered:

I hope by the time you get this, you will have some good news. Gee, mom, I don't know what to say except I hope and pray Dale is safe wherever he is. It was sure grand to talk to you and Darlene.

Del is studying. He says for you and dad to keep your chins up and don't worry too much. Everything will be alright.

I guess there isn't any use for any of us to tell each other not to worry because we will anyway. All any of us can do is hope and pray for the best.

Love,
Evelyn and Delbert

Doris, unaware that Dale was missing, had written him a V-letter.

Dear Dale,

We have not heard from you for about three weeks but probably will before too long. I sent a Christmas card and Warren and I both wrote letters in it some time ago, but it was not a V-letter so it may not get to you.

I would take some pictures and send some once in a while but can't get any film. Mom sent me a picture of the service flag with its five stars in her last letter. It looks really swell.

Junior writes the cutest letters. I hope you hear from him as you would get a bang from the way he puts things.

I'm going to let you in on a secret. We haven't told anyone yet, but we are going to have a boy (we hope) next May. Have you any suggestions for a name? Warren doesn't like "Roger" and you can guess why.

Write when you can,
Doris

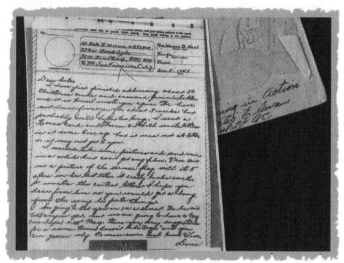

DORIS'S V-LETTER WAS RETURNED UNOPENED,
MARKED "MISSING," DECEMBER 1943

The next day, Doris learned that Dale was missing. She sent her folks a telegram to tell them not to worry. She wrote Dale again:

Dear Dale,

I am praying you get this and the one I sent a couple of days ago, too. You have just GOT to be okay.

About noon yesterday I got a letter from Mom that they received a telegram that you were lost. But we know you will be found. Mom got the telegram on her birthday.

When Warren came home, he had our V-letter of November 23rd. I had hoped it was written after the date on the telegram so I could wire home. I did wire them not to worry.

God bless you, Dale. And all the good luck to you.

Doris

Doris wrote her folks that she had just finished another V-letter to Dale and had gotten one from him dated November 23rd.

Dear Mom and Dad,

I sure was hoping the V-letter I got from Dale was dated after November 27th, but no such luck. I'm glad he got your package, Mom, and I'm glad I happened to write when I did. I hope he heard from Junior, but as to Danny, I would bet he didn't. Dale would really like to hear from him more than anyone.

I have been forgetting to tell Darlene she can have that green jumper she asked for. You can give it to her the next time you see her. I am supposed to tell her something I want of hers, but the only thing I can think of, I'm gonna have of my own in May. Surprised? Probably not, as you kind of hinted in one of your letters, Mom. I'm tired of keeping it a secret, especially when I think about it so much.

Keep me informed about everyone and don't either of you worry about anything as it only makes things worse.

Love,
Doris

Another letter arrived from Delbert and Evelyn:

Dear Mom and Dad,

You two don't work too hard now. And take good care of yourselves. We will carry on, won't we? With courage, hope, and prayer to guide us.

We sure enjoyed those pictures of Sam and our Richard. Like to have a picture of our folks, too! How about it? Keep your chins up, Dad 'n' Mom. We will all be together soon. God is on our side. We can't lose.

Evelyn and I think it best to not say anything to the two younger boys so as not to worry them. I'm sure we will hear some good news soon. And please try not to worry yourselves sick. We know how you feel, and it is terrible not to be able to do anything for you. So keep your chins up and keep praying. I'm sure everything will be alright; it just has to be. We are glad Darlene is with you.

Love,
Delbert and Evelyn

Darlene certainly was a comfort to her folks during the war years. She stayed with them a few days after they got the hard news, and little Richard kept them all entertained.

When Donald wrote home, he asked his folks about the telegram.

Mom and Dad,

What were the exact words of the telegram? It's possible that Dale could have bailed out or crash landed. Or he could have been forced down in the dense tropics. If that happened, it will take time for him to make his way back to a base. In this case, the chances are good that he could be with some of the rest of his crew.

The tropics are bad for rainstorms, too. Maybe they lost their base and landed somewhere else. They could be making their way back and it will take quite a bit of time to do that.

I got a letter from Dale written on November 24th. He told me about the Christmas package and how good the American candy tasted. He told me about being a fifth of the way through his missions and how he was planning on getting into a new, medium attack bomber if he could. He also said that I guessed right as to his location when he first went down there. He was in Australia for a couple of months before he moved up into New Guinea. I just can't help but think he's okay.

It seems like quite a while to us since he's gone missing, but time goes by fast for a man trying to buck the jungle. A month would be a short time to get back to a base, even with the help of natives.

Do you remember Francis Love? He graduated with Doris. He is a pilot and went missing in action twice in New Guinea. Both times he made it back to his base.

One of these days those Japs are going to feel the full fury of the fleet out there in the Pacific. I get so damn mad at times, I think I'll always be hunting Japs.

I got a visit from our old neighbor from Minburn, Harold Snyder. It was nice to visit with people from home.

Love,
Donald and Rose

Dallas County, Iowa
Christmas, 1943

Leora

Letters continued back and forth between family members. Leora
continued to write to Dale, always hopeful for the best.

Dear Dale,

*I did a big washing as this is Monday. Dad has a big load of oats and
corn ready to grind when the grinder comes. Dad said to tell you the John
Deere runs fine, and he is getting so he can run it pretty good.*

*I expect Sam, Darlene, and Richard will be over on Christmas. I wish
you were all to be here on that day. We are so anxious to get word from you
that you are okay. I hope you and your pals have a nice Christmas. We will
be thinking of you, as we do all the time, and pray for your safety.*

Love,
Mom

Marfa, Texas
Christmas, 1943
Doris

Doris's November 16th V-mail letter to Dale telling him that she was expecting a baby was returned and stamped "Missing." It was also printed by hand on the back:

HQ 823ʳᵈ Bomb. Sq. 38ᵗʰ Bomb. GP.
To: Commanding General USAFFE,
APO 501, Missing in Action,
For the Squadron Commander,
Curtis E. Swan, 1ˢᵗ Lt., A.C., Adjutant

Once Doris received this, she wrote to Junior and Danny right away to tell them about Dale. She couldn't imagine them getting the news by having a letter returned like the one she just received. She told her mom that she would have been shocked if she hadn't known, so she hoped this was the right thing to do.

Earlham, Madison County, Iowa
Christmas, 1943
Darlene

Darlene also continued to write to Dale.

Dearest Dale,

Hope this finds you safe and bombing to victory. We listen to the radio news so close and hope it's as good as it sounds.

Our Christmas is going to be as happy as possible this year, but we're all planning to be together next year and really feel the Christmas spirit. There really is a God and everyone prays to him more than ever at this time.

Say, Dale, maybe Mom has told you—Richard is going to have two cousins this spring. Doris and Warren are expecting a precious bundle in May, and Delbert and Evelyn in June. We're all so thrilled.

Love and Prayers,
Darlene

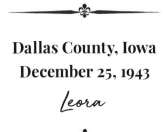

Dallas County, Iowa
December 25, 1943

Leora

Dear Dale,

Hope this letter finds you all right after the world's Christmas Day. Of course, it is the 26th over there.

Dad and I listened to a world broadcast last night. New Guinea was one place they broadcast from. Sure would have liked to hear your voice.

Dad and I are alone today—doesn't seem much like it is Christmas with you boys and girls all away. And there is no snow on the ground. We know it didn't seem like Christmas to you either, but be of good cheer, as everyone all over the world expects to be home for next Christmas. We sure pray to God it will be so.

We are anxious to hear from you that you are all right.

Love and Best of Luck,
Mom and Dad

Stillwater, Oklahoma
Christmas, 1943

Junior

Still unaware of the news about Dale, Junior wrote home.

Mom and Dad,

Got the pictures from home. Joe makes me want to reach right out and pet him! The one of Dad holding the gun with Spats and Joe makes me think of home. A picture is better than a letter itself.

I am bunking with a farmer who had a John Deere. We do a lot of talking on the subject.

Stillwater is about the size of Perry. We went to a wild-west show. Boy, these old Oklahomans sure like the shooting and the flying dust. I will have to admit that I do too!

Oklahoma A&M stands for Agricultural and Mechanical. We passed some hog pens the other day and the guys held their noses. I just laughed and said it reminded me of home! Ha!

I got your present. I'm telling you, the figs and nuts really tasted good, although they were devoured in about 15 minutes! It reminded me of the good old times when we went to Perry and invaded the Thriftway store. No doubt that's where you got them.

How's it going on the farm? Boy, how I would like to be there on the bottom today. Might get in on a little pheasant or fox hunting if I were back. You know, I could even stand the hog dust, too! Ha!

Take Care and Merry Christmas,
Junior

Then Junior received Doris's note about Dale.

Mom and Dad,

It gave me a damn sickish feeling in my stomach and throat. Of course he will be found. New Guinea is a big place and has a heavy jungle, so he will be found. I don't want you to worry any, although I know damn well you will.

Keep busy and chins up,
Junior

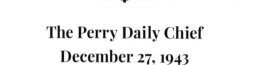

The Perry Daily Chief
December 27, 1943
Lieut. Dale Wilson Listed Missing
Minburn Youth Had Been Serving as a Bomber Pilot
In Southwest Pacific

An Associated Press dispatch today from Washington, D.C., reported that the war department had listed second Lieut. Dale R. Wilson of Minburn as missing in action in the southwest Pacific.

Mr. and Mrs. C.D. Wilson, who live on a farm southwest of Minburn, had been notified by the war department earlier this month, but the public announcement was not made until today.

A letter from the war department said the family would be kept informed of developments and both Mr. and Mrs. Wilson have hopes that their son is safe. Quite a number of times, men are reported missing and then turn up safe and sound after a few weeks.

Lieut. Wilson, 22 years old, was trained as an army bomber pilot and received his wings and commission at Roswell, N.M.

Mr. and Mrs. Wilson have four other sons in the service. They are Delbert, 28, first class electrical machinist's mate and stationed with the navy at Washington, D.C.; Donald, 27, chief electrician's mate, also with the navy in Washington; Daniel, 20, in the army air training at Tucson, Ariz.; and Junior, 18, in army air corps college training at Stillwater, Okla.

Dallas County, Iowa
December 29, 1943
Clabe and Leora

The Wilsons received a letter from Headquarters, Army Air Forces:

Dear Mr. Wilson,

Under date of December 3rd, The Adjutant General notified you that your son, Second Lieutenant Dale R. Wilson, had been reported missing in action, over New Guinea, since November 27th.

Further information has been received indicating that Lieutenant Wilson was a crew member of a B-25, (Mitchell), bomber which participated in a combat mission over the island of New Guinea on November 27th. Full details are not available, but the report indicates that during this mission, your son's plane sustained damage from enemy antiaircraft fire and was seen to fall into the water. The report further states that this occurred at about 11:30 a.m. off the Northern coast of New Guinea.

Due to the necessity for military security, it is regretted that the names of those who were in the plane, and the names and addresses of their next of kin, may not be furnished at the present time.

The above facts constitute all of the information presently available. The great anxiety caused you by failure to receive more details concerning your son's disappearance is fully realized. Please be assured that any additional information received will be conveyed to you immediately.

Trying to keep up the hope and normalcy, Leora wrote to Dale again.

Dear Dale,

Wherever you are, we all hope you are all right. We are anxious to get word that you are safe.

Dad hasn't had any good hunting weather—no snow to track anything. He and the dogs go out with the gun anyway once in a while, mostly just for the walk.

Darlene, Sam, and Richard were here on Christmas in the evening and stayed over Sunday. Richard does a lot of jabbering now—just like he was telling something so funny and then he laughs. He had us laughing too! Sam made him a cute little chair and Darlene painted it red. He looks cute sitting on it—when he sits, anyway. He sure doesn't sit still very long. He's a busy little boy.

This war may be over before another Christmas. We pray to God it is, so we can settle down in peace over the world. A war-weary world.

Love and best of luck to you always, Dale. And God Bless you.
Mom and Dad

1943 ended with the Wilson family members scattered all over the globe. Both oldest brothers were married and living in Washington, D.C. Danny was in Arizona for Basic Training. Junior was in Oklahoma, just beginning his Air Corps stint. Doris was also married, living in Texas where Warren was instructing cadets. Both Delbert's wife and Doris were expecting babies. Only Darlene was living nearby.

And Dale, missing in action, in a strange, far-away place—New Guinea.

CHAPTER 10

Early 1944

Dallas County, Iowa
January 1944

Leora

Dear Son Dale,

This is my first letter in 1944. We hope you are well and getting along alright wherever you are. We are all so anxious to hear from you.

Dad and I are alone today, so I am writing letters. Dad has been over west in the fields to see how the horses and cattle are getting along. We've had a little snow, but not enough for your dad to track game. Smokey Joe likes to come in the house when it is cold and lie under the cook stove, just like Spats did.

I expect Danny is ready to go to Advanced Training now. I'm anxious to know where he will go.

I'll write to you again in a few days, Dale boy. Until then, lots of love to you.

God Bless You,
Mom and Dad

Washington, D.C.
Early 1944
Evelyn

Dear Mom and Dad,

Delbert has a hard time talking about Dale. He's had some nightmares lately. One night, it woke me up. Del was crying in his sleep and it took me five minutes to wake him. He was sobbing as if his heart was broken.

I guess you and Dad get pretty lonesome after having all those big boys around you nearly all the time. They will be back someday, Mom, so just keep your chin up. And imagine—your family will be much larger, and you and Dad will be grandparents a few more times. I wonder if Doris will beat us!

We know film is hard to come by during this war, but we managed to get two rolls for you folks. Delbert wants you to take some pictures and send one of Dad on the tractor and feeding the hogs. He'd also like one of you feeding your flock, Mom.

We'll keep writing and praying for the best.

Love,
Evelyn and Delbert

Delbert

Delbert had written Dale's commanding officer asking for details of his last mission. He received a reply from Major Holland Legg and enclosed it with the letter Evelyn had written.

"In answer to your letter of 13 December 1943, I am able to furnish you with the following facts surrounding the incident which resulted in your brother being listed as missing in action.

"Your brother was engaged in action against the enemy while flying his plane over enemy held territory on the north coast of New Guinea on the date specified in your letter. After the objective had been achieved, the airplane was seen to suddenly lose its flying speed just as the formation was passing the shoreline and heading out to sea. The plane struck the water but seemed to bounce off and continue its flight in a controlled glide at a reduced speed for three-fourths of a mile, finally coming to rest without apparent serious damage to the bulk of the airplane. The crews of the remaining two airplanes in the flight watched the disabled airplane for a period of twenty or thirty seconds, or until it passed from their view. No person reported seeing the men in your brother's crew leave their airplane, although it was partially afloat when last seen. If it were within your brother's comrades' premise to offer hope that he may be safe, they would not hesitate to do so. But as these are all the facts we have, we hesitate to offer that hope."

Dear Mom and Dad ,

The way Donald and I see it, it sounds like Dale might have been forced down in the jungle, flying low with no chance to use their parachutes. We figure they'd been shooting at Japanese barges and supply ships with a three-inch cannon. After losing speed and hitting the water, once they knew they couldn't make it, they surely had plenty of time to prepare their equipment for ditching. The plane must have still been in good shape or it wouldn't have stayed afloat as long as it did. Dale and his crew probably made it ashore and were slowly making their way through the jungle.

They carry knives and .45's. Four or five fellows have a better chance than one fellow alone. He will make it out, we know. It may be quite a while, but he will. Lots of fellows have come out even after months.

Chins up,
Delbert

Dallas County, Iowa
Early 1944

Leora

After receiving Delbert and Evelyn's letters, Leora wrote to Doris about the reply Del had gotten from Dale's commanding officer. She copied the whole thing by hand for them, and also made copies for Danny and Junior using carbon paper for some of the pages.

Dear Doris and Warren,

It made us feel better to know the circumstances and what Delbert and Donald thought. It gives us hope that they might just be making their way in the jungle.

We figure they would have time to get their equipment ready to get out in their rubber raft and life jackets they wear all the time. I think the letter from Dale's officer said that it happened around 11:30 a.m., so there was plenty of daylight left, but they may have waited 'til dark to try and go ashore. We believe we'll get good word from him soon.

Only three letters I sent Dale have been returned. They must be holding his mail for him.

Write when you can.
Mom

Leora kept busy gathering eggs every day. She had about seventy-five dozen ready to take to Perry to sell at thirty cents a dozen.

When she wasn't busy with chores, she wrote to all of her children, including Dale. Leora wrote to him every few days.

Dear Son Dale,

We hope and pray you are alright wherever you are. We are so anxious to get a letter from you telling us you are okay.

Love,
Mom

Marana, Arizona
Early 1944
Danny

Danny arrived at Williams Field on January 7, 1944—his dad's birthday. The first things to catch his eye were the grass, palm trees, and the P-38s whistling around. Danny wrote all about his training and the airplanes. But the focus of his letter was his reaction to the news that Dale was missing.

Dear Mom and Dad,

I got Doris's letter in the middle of instrument training. You know what she told me. I saw 'missing in action' the very first thing—it's like my eyes went straight to those words. I hoped and prayed enough now that I really believe they haven't got Dale. He's just 'missing' for a while, like they said 'missing in action' meant.

Dale's the best and toughest guy in the world. If he's in those damn jungles, I know he'll make it back okay. Those damn rats can't get by with a halfway job with Dale. I hope they find him and then I want to get through training and get over there with him. Both of us could make those devils die and go to hell for their damned emperor. Dale's my ideal guy and my ambition is to be with him.

All of us who flew AT-6s are ordered to Williams Field near Phoenix to train in twin-engine fighters. It's within sight of Marana, so I'll take Primary, Basic, and Advanced all within sight of each other.

I'm sure glad you wrote in the last letter, Dad. I know damn well you've got more than you can do to get it all done. Knock off what you can and go hunting. How are you doing driving the tractor and Plymouth? Do you have to haul water to the pigs in barrels? Aw, hell, the pigs are hogs now and can get their own water. Seen any fox, Dad? Let me know.

Thank you both for the Christmas package. The figs and nuts reminded me of going to Perry. The handkerchiefs and tie have come in handy.

That is all for now. Let me know when you hear from Dale.

Danny

CHAPTER 11

Spring 1944

Williams Field, Arizona
March 1944
Danny

Williams Field, Advanced Flying School, Chandler, Arizona, announced the graduation of Class 44-C Pilots, Sunday morning, March twelfth, Nineteen hundred and forty-four. Second Lieutenant Daniel S. Wilson was awarded his commission and pilot's wings.

Danny didn't get a furlough right away like Dale did. They were to get shipping orders when they cleared Williams Field, but were delayed. They'd also been assured of ten days' delay enroute, but their orders just said to report to Victorville, California, for Transition the next day. They did so but were rather low on morale when they arrived.

Dear Mom and Dad,

I got checked out in the AT-6 after three landings (just required procedure) and fifteen of us went the next day into an instrument squadron. We flew the radio beams. All instrument flying is done under the hood in the back seat. Anyway, I had to fly, think, scheme, dream, and sweat for about two weeks.

Now that we have our wings, I'm told we are pioneers. Seven P-39s, called Airacobras, are here from combat at Guadalcanal, and later models are being ferried in. So, here's three things I can tell you about these planes. . . . Dad, I know you'll get a kick out of this. I can roll down the window and spit over the wingtip, it has a high-flying speed, and it has a gliding angle of a brick!

I've written to Dale and my letters were returned. I'd give anything and everything if he could be found alive. I want to fight the Japs. Flying this type of plane, I think I'll get to. If he's alive or not, every stinking bastard I run into is the one that did it. And if I see a Jap bail out, wounded, or any stinking on the ground—they will be no exception.

I'll never be taken prisoner by any of them.

Danny

Dallas County, Iowa
Spring 1944
Leora

Dear Son Dale,

Hope this finds you well and alright, wherever you are. We are all anxious to get good word from you.

Danny didn't get to come home at the time he got his wings on March 12th. He went to Victorville in California. He called us long distance last night and said he was going to try and get leave in a month or two. He said he had so much to tell and show us. We were sure disappointed he didn't get to come home now, but we just have to take things as they come in these times, and hope for better times which we are sure will be. And before long, too.

Doris and Warren are on their way. They will get to Des Moines at 6:20 a.m. if the train is on time. I guess Warren's brother is going after them. He is home on leave. He got his wings the same day Dan did.

Dad has been cutting wood in the timber. I'm getting ready for baby chicks April 2nd.

Love and best wishes to you Dale boy. And God bless you.
Mom

Wearing a cotton maternity top, Doris washed up the breakfast dishes. Warren had already returned to Marfa. "Mom, it's so good to be home, out in the country again."

"It's wonderful having you here," said her mother. "And your baby will be born in our healthy Iowa. From what you and Junior tell me about Texas, it's all cactus and dust."

"It does seem healthier here, but I wonder what to do about my poor, swelled feet and hands!"

"Rest is a good idea. Get some sunshine and fresh air."

"I can help you in the garden, but first I need to get the footlocker back to Warren in case he needs to pack in a hurry. Maybe Dad can take me to ship it about the time your mail comes."

An order had come for fifteen Marfa instructors with a year's service and over one thousand flying hours to go to Roswell for four engine training in B-17s. But of the ten men in his class, Warren and one other were not on the list. The others only had a twenty-four-hour notice to leave. They'd heard that fifteen pilots would be sent out every month, fly B-17s for a month, then train in B-29s—the Army's new bomber.

Doris had mentioned to Delbert and Evelyn about the swelling in her hands and feet.

Delbert wrote back:

Dear Doris,

I've been reading up on babies and I consider myself an authority on the subject. If you know of anyone who is need of advice, please inform them to address their letters to D.G. Wilson EM1/c, M.D. of B. and P.W., Washington, D.C., U.S.A. Ha!

On the subject of swelling hands and feet—probably due to a number of things. Number one: You probably are going to have a baby, yes? Well, then there you are, that's it. You see, there ain't too much to being an authority! All kidding aside, it is due mainly to a strain on a person's kidneys. You probably should watch your diet—not too much sugar or meats. And drink plenty of fluids to keep the system flushed.

Your expert on all things pregnancy related,
Delbert

The Minburn timber was in full bloom. Clabe and his dog Spats walked up the dusty lane with the mail. He waved to a neighbor driving by.

"Who do we know in Reno, Nevada?" Clabe asked as he brought the mail inside.

"No one that I know of." Leora and Doris were near the back door.

"Let's see what this is all about." Doris took the envelope and tore off one end.

Dear Mr. Wilson,

Last night I had the unusual fortune to get a foreign broadcast on the short-wave band of the radio. It was from Japan. They gave your address and the message that your son, Dale Ross Wilson, was rescued from his plane and is now a prisoner on the island of Wewak. Perhaps other Americans also heard this broadcast and notified you as well. If not, I am glad to be of service to you.

May the Lord give you courage.

Nancy Street

Leora began to cry. Clabe held her as Doris joined them, still holding the letter. She wiped tears with the back of her hand. "What a relief to know that he's alive!"

"How did this woman get that information?" Clabe wondered.

"I think there are people who listen to these broadcasts all the time," said Doris. "I didn't realize they wrote people. This is wonderful if it's true."

Leora brushed tears away with her apron. "We need to take this to the Red Cross office in Perry. Maybe they can learn more or get a message to our Dale boy."

Before the Wilsons could get to Perry, two more letters about the short-wave message came from people who'd heard it in Seattle and Los Angeles. Now they were ready to believe that Dale was still alive.

Leora wrote to thank those who'd notified them. She was thankful that Dale was still alive, but worried that four months was a long time to be a prisoner of Japan. She hoped and prayed that Dale was okay and that they would receive word directly from him.

The Perry Daily Chief, April 4, 1944:

Mr. and Mrs. Clabe D. Wilson of Minburn, whose son, Lieut. Dale Ross Wilson was reported missing in action in the Pacific war theatre some time ago, have heard that a Jap broadcast last week said Lieut. Wilson was a prisoner. According to messages to the Wilsons from several persons on the west coast who picked up the Jap short-wave broadcast, the enemy radio said Lieut. Wilson was rescued after his plane was shot down in the sea. The report added that he is a prisoner of war of the imperial Japanese army at Wewak, New Guinea. Mr. and Mrs. Wilson have received no official word, other than their son is missing.

Dallas County, Iowa
Spring, 1944
Danny

Danny finally got a furlough home, arriving in Iowa at the Boone train station in the middle of the night. He caught a ride as far as Ogden, then called home around 2:00 a.m. for his folks to come get him.

It rained the weekend Sam, Darlene, and little Richard came over to see him.

"All this mud sure makes it hard to go anywhere," Leora said, "but we sure want to get a good picture of you in Perry in your uniform, Danny boy."

"Let's get that done right away. If it stops raining, I'd like to get some plowing done for Dad while I'm here."

But it kept raining. Then Danny got a telegram cutting his leave eight days short, ordering him to Salinas, California.

The family was able to get to Perry to have Danny's picture taken before he needed to leave.

It finally cleared off on the day he was to depart, and Darlene came with Richard. "Let's get some snapshots of you and your sisters," Leora suggested.

They took photos of Danny with his folks, Danny with Darlene and little Richard tucked in his arm like a football, and one with Spats in it as well. Doris stepped into the last photo, tucking herself behind Danny so her "condition" wouldn't show.

During the picture-taking, a meadowlark's song rippled from a nearby fencepost. Danny remarked that the meadowlark was his favorite bird. He left for California April 27, after just eight days at home.

LT. DANIEL S. WILSON, PERRY, IOWA, APRIL 1944

SISTERS DARLENE SCAR AND DORIS
NEAL WITH DANNY WILSON, HOLDING
DARLENE'S SON, RICHARD. A MEADOW-
LARK SANG DURING THE PHOTO TAKING.
DANNY SAID IT WAS HIS FAVORITE BIRD.

Salinas, California

Danny

Dear Mom and Dad,

I'm writing this on the top deck of a bunk in a barracks that is longer than (but similar to) the building by the barn that you use for the hens.

I rode all the way to Frisco on that train car that I got on in Boone. When we got to Omaha, more soldiers and people got on than were seats. It was that way for the rest of the trip, with even more getting on at Cheyenne and Ogden. Several of my buddies were in the same car as me. Four of us had to sleep practically on top of each other.

We went across Great Salt Lake, across Nevada, and shortly after starting into California, we ran into the most beautiful country I'd seen in the west. Mountain pine forests, grass, wild flowers, and farms and homes were in the valleys. Sacramento is right in it and I'm sure we passed the Army air field at which Dale was before embarkation.

We took a ferry from Oakland to Frisco and passed under Oakland Bay Bridge where I saw my first Navy warship—a cruiser.

I expect to be here about a month taking classes, target practice, and to get my veins diluted with all the shots I need to go overseas. Salinas is about the size of Boone, Iowa. It's spread out, green, and even has meadowlarks.

Danny

Chico, California
May 1944
Danny

Dear Mom and Dad,

I'm in Chico now. It's about a hundred miles north of Sacramento and near the foothills of the mountains. We get to do a lot of flying in P-39s and P-63s. Much of the flying is in combat formation. It's like a real airshow here. The planes come in from the distance with an increasing rumbling and whistling sound, and then peel-off over the field.

It's May 13th today—The birthday of the best guy I know. I hope to get good news about him being liberated. I heard that MacArthur was bypassing places in the South Pacific and letting the POWs starve into submission. I'm afraid Dale is going to be about starved to death if he does make it out of there. Don figures he'll be down in there again before long. I hope I am too.

So, I'll be an uncle again soon. Probably to a Wilson or a Neal. . . which one first?

I'm sending home $100 to save for that place you'll have after this war.

Danny

CHAPTER 12

Summer 1944

Stillwater, Oklahoma
Summer, 1944

Junior

Dear Mom and Dad,

I wish I was back there in the hog-dust again. I will never forget those long-nosed hogs slicing their way through the ragweed.

I hope you can handle everything, Dad. Once this war is over, we can all buy the place of our dreams.

The other morning I had some good ol' wheat! I ate it with the same kind of tablespoons you have had ever since I can remember. Boy it was good. So was the reminder of home.

Stillwater has a skating rink, the movies, and places to drink beer. Since I don't drink or skate, I've been catching a lot of shows. All of them are at least a year old and westerns. I guess the Oklahomans like their westerns.

Junior

San Antonio, Texas
Summer, 1944
Junior

Dear Mom and Dad,

Well, I'm getting farther away from home with every move I make. We had to be in quarantine for fifteen days when we got here. We filled our time with physical training, drills, and guard detail.

I'll bet Iowa is really getting pretty this time of year. You can smell it, see it, and feel the spring and summer in Iowa, but you can't in the southwest. San Antone is a wide-open, dirty city. There's dives, holes, joints, and dens all over the place. I went to the Alamo once and they turned it into a beer joint. It sure is a money-grabbing place. They display the Texas flag much more than the Stars and Stripes.

I am officially an aviation cadet. I am beginning to see the things Dale and Dan went through. If I fail any tests now, I'm washing out. They used to just send you back a class. I'll probably be a gunner before long.

After the war I might become a physical educator, along with flying, farming and a few other occupations. Ha!

Dad, I hope you are getting along okay with the farming. I sure wish I could be back on the John Deere helping you.

I'm glad to hear that Dale is still alive. I don't like the stories I read of the things happening near Wewak. I hope they are feeding him at least a bowl of rice a week. You and I know he will come out of this okay. If anyone can, it's Dale.

Junior

Dallas County, Iowa
June 1944
Doris

Spring moving into summer is a beautiful time of year in Iowa—blue and purple violets, the frothy white of plum thickets, songs of migrating birds and an earthy, woodsy aroma.

"It's a perfect day to hang out the washing," Doris told her mother. "I need to get the baby's things ready for the hospital. Baby 'Bruce' and I can soak up some healthy sunshine."

After the wash was all on the line, Leora and Doris walked up the hill to where Clabe was plowing. They took him a cool drink, taking their time hiking through the timber. On their way back to the house, the two picked wildflowers for the kitchen table. Sounds of blue jays calling their warnings and mourning doves softly cooing provided background music as they enjoyed the afternoon.

One late spring day, Doris and her mother helped Clabe get a couple of sows penned in. The grunting beasts didn't want to give up their little weed patches for a hog house with clean straw. With a little maneuvering and a bit of persuasion, they finally got them in.

"Isn't it interesting?" she wrote to Warren. "Fourteen sows have little pigs, two cows have calves so far, and two cats have kittens. Guess maybe I'll be next!"

The Redfield Review announced: "Born to Lieut. and Mrs. Warren Neal of Marfa, Texas, a baby girl was born on Sunday, June 4th at the Dexter

clinic. Lieut. Neal arrived from Marfa last Friday, where he is an instructor at the Army Air base. Mrs. Neal has been visiting since March at
the home of her parents, Mr. and Mrs. Clabe Wilson of Minburn."

Doris and Warren named their baby "Joy."

Washington, D.C.
June 1944
Delbert

Dear Mom and Dad,

Gee, I'll bet everyone is excited around there! Doris told us it seems just like Christmas to her. What a present!

Evelyn is miserable with swollen legs and high blood pressure. She is getting tired of waiting for the baby to arrive. The doctor ordered her to bedrest and to stay off her feet.

My jaw is still swollen from having wisdom teeth pulled. I'm taking sulfa for an infected gland. I only have two weeks of Interior Communication School left, then I'm not sure where I'll be next.

Donald stopped by. His ship, the "Hancock," is about to head out for six weeks of shakedown training off Trinidad and Venezuela. They will conduct battle practice, antiaircraft practice, and practicing with a new aircraft squadron. By this time next year, we will have such a force over there, we can go right in and flatten Japan itself. Their sun will be sinking by this time in 1945. I don't think Germany will last later than Christmas this year. Sure is the most terrible slugging match going on in the history of the world right now. Thank God for our air power.

Delbert

When Evelyn went into labor, Delbert had fallen asleep with an ice pack on his jaw. Their landlady had stopped by, so she ended up taking Evelyn to the hospital.

A newspaper clipping read:

Mr. and Mrs. Delbert Wilson of Washington, D.C. announce the birth of a daughter, Leora Darlene, on June 15th. This is the third grandchild of Mr. and Mrs. Clabe Wilson of Minburn. Delbert, who is an electrician's mate 1-c has been attending Interior Communication School in Washington, D.C. and will graduate June 26th.

Delbert was accepted for Submarine School at New London, Connecticut, so they'd be moving. In fact, when he learned they wanted Electrical Interior Communication men to set up mechanical and electrical problems for the "boots," he applied for the job of running an "Attack Teacher" there. This would mean a year of shore duty.

Evelyn hoped that by the time Delbert's time was over at the submarine school, the worst of the war would be over, and that Danny wouldn't even have to go overseas.

And that they would hear something about Dale.

San Antonio, Texas
June 1944
Junior

Dear Mom and Dad,

Looks like the Wilson tribe has increased considerably in the last month! I see Del and Evelyn have given their girl your name, Mom.

How's the farming, Dad? Wish I was back in the cornfield getting some Iowa sun. I can just hear the green corn leaves slapping against the axle of the John Deere. Don't worry about the cockle-burrs and the wet spots. There's more feed wasted by leaving it on the plate than there is in leaving it in the field.

I'm able to keep up on the news. I sure hope they clean up the Wewak area soon. They are raiding off the coast of New Guinea near Wewak. I wish Dale was doing the raiding instead of being raided.

Here's some more money to put on the pile and save for a little farm of our own. Or spend it however you want. I can live on less than five bucks a month, so I don't need it.

Junior

Curtis Field, Brady, Texas
June 1944

Dear Mom and Dad,

I started to fly here at Curtis Field. I like it better every time I go up. It's fun to fly low, see shadows of the mesquite bushes, and fly over cattle country. They treat the cadets like gentlemen here, but the washout rate is pretty high. All I can do is try hard and do my best.

The officers are swell here and the chow is pretty good. I can have all the milk I want for breakfast. I sure would like to sink my tusks into an ear of sweet corn dripping with butter. We get canned corn about every dinner, but it is dark and tastes a lot like a tin can.

I went to a rodeo. They probably had some pretty good shows in the good-ol' days. Texans think they are hot stuff when they put on their boots and get on a horse. If you are from Texas, you're a hero!

I sure hope the war will be over in another year. I read in the official Air Force magazine that Wewak has been in our hands for quite a while. We put an air-blockade around Wewak and the Japs had to evacuate. I surely hope they didn't starve the prisoners.

Don't you folks work too hard during the hot weather, now. Be sure to eat lots of greens and drink plenty of water.

Junior

---❖---

Curtis Field, Brady, Texas
Summer, 1944

Junior

---❖---

Dear Mom and Dad,

Thanks for the pictures! Mom, you sure look good. Of course, so does everyone. Richard sure has changed a lot. He really is becoming some kind of boy. In a few more years, he can start on the weights! Ha!

Can you take a picture from up on the hill to across the river? Or from the house and down across the bayou toward the river? I can just about remember every tree around the Minburn farm, they are all so pretty. The only trees in Texas are scrawny mesquite bushes or some other haggard-looking thing. I can really appreciate a spreading elm or just a second-growth burr-oak. Well, enough of the dreaming!

Soloing was fun. I can fly easier without an instructor with me. After I first soloed, my buddies threw me in the shower with my clothes on!

Dad, I hope you can write me a few lines. Write anything. About the hogs or whatever you want.

I wish we would get some word from the South Pacific.

Junior

SISTERS DARLENE, HOLDING
RICHARD, AND DORIS, HOLDING
MONTH-OLD JOY. MINBURN,
JULY 4, 1944

Chico, California
Summer, 1944
Danny

Dear Mom and Dad,

The pictures from home sure are swell. Everyone looks so good. I'm going to keep the one of you and the chickens, Mom. Somehow, it seems the best one.

I saw seven jack-rabbits while on safety officer duty. I had two flare pistols and had that urge to go rabbit hunting. I knew I'd catch hell and be written up if I did.

They are bringing in more P-38Ls every few days and taking out some of the P-63s. The L is the latest model. It's big for a fighter plane. I might be in Chico a little longer.

Dad, it's okay that you're laying by some of the corn. Mom says you have one of the best fields. I can see that, because you always have. You're one of the best farmers, that's for sure. You deserve a place of your own where you can manage the work as you want.

Danny

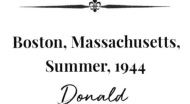

Boston, Massachusetts, Summer, 1944
Donald

Navy men were given assignments after graduation according to their grades. Donald had third choice of the Chiefs. He chose the brand-new carrier USS *Hancock* in Boston, figuring it would be a while before commissioning. So he and Rose moved to the Boston area.

The carrier held seven weeks of "shakedown" practice drills off Chesapeake Bay and into the Caribbean.

Dear Mom and Dad,

The shakedown training was a continuous grind. All the work was below the decks, so I didn't get a suntan this time. But it wasn't safe topside with the pilots training.

Some of the crew couldn't take the grind and were transferred. In fact, the other Chief Electrician's Mate was one of them, so now I am the Senior Chief Electrician's Mate on this brand-new aircraft carrier. All this means, though, is that I am to make out the watch list for the division, on top of my other duties.

When we were in the Port of Spain, I bought Rose a bottle of Chanel No. 5 and three pair of silk hose. At least I hope they were real. I paid $3.50 a pair.

Right now I am taking life easy after the shakedown. The ship is getting alterations. I expect to be in the Philippines by September. That's really a hot spot since it's getting close to Japan. I expect to be in on some raids in Japan one of these days. I look for a big surface battle out there any day now.

Donald

Rose attended the formal commissioning of the USS *Hancock* and, when the ship left Boston with Donald aboard, she took the train to the West Coast to meet him. She stopped by the Wilson farm in Iowa for a short visit.

Somehow, even after sending telegrams, they missed connections in California. Rose, broken-hearted after Donald's ship had left the West Coast without her seeing him, headed to Aberdeen, Washington where her father lived.

Dear Mom and Dad,

Ya, Dad, the rats as you call them, are catching it. I sure hope Dale has been moved from Wewak or he would be starving.

Your letters are my main source of entertainment on this ship. News here is scarce. At least the news I can write about.

Take good care of yourselves and hope for the best. One of these days it will all end, and we'll have a reunion.

Donald

Marfa, Texas
Summer, 1944
Doris

Before Doris left Iowa, she and her folks looked at an acreage for sale a mile south of Perry. It was just five acres and seemed like a bargain. They bought it that afternoon. It needed a lot of fixing up, but Clabe and Leora were excited about finally having a place of their own. The money their sons sent home helped them to buy the property.

Warren made it back to get Doris and they loaded everything into the used Chevy he'd bought in May. Together, their little family of three headed for Texas.

WARREN, DORIS, AND BABY JOY READY TO LEAVE IN THEIR 1939 CHEVY FOR MARFA, TEXAS. AUGUST 1944

On their way, they wanted to see Junior at the base. It was too late the night they arrived, so they drove out the next morning. They were able to locate him right away as he had one of the most athletic builds on the field.

The Neals experienced some car trouble on their way south. Warren hoped the right rear tire on their Chevy would hold up on the trip, but partway through, he had to put the spare tire on. It was a struggle to keep the spare from going flat, and they couldn't replace it as rubber was needed for the war effort.

Unfortunately, that wasn't the only car trouble they had. The gas gauge wasn't working correctly and about ten miles from the base, they ran out of gas. It was about 9:00 at night and Warren had to leave Doris and the baby in the dark car while he hitch-hiked to Marfa to get fuel for the remainder of their trip.

Doris spent five days unpacking their belongings in the church rooms they rented.

Reported in *The Perry Daily Chief:*

Mrs. Donald W. Wilson left last week from Ames for San Francisco, California, after a two week visit at the home of Mr. and Mrs. Clabe Wilson. She went to meet her husband, CEM Donald W. Wilson, who arrived on the west coast with his ship from Boston, Mass.

Lt. Warren D. Neal arrived by plane at Des Moines last week for a ten-day leave. His wife and little daughter Joy accompanied him home by car to Marfa, Texas. They left Thursday evening. Mrs. Neal and baby had visited at the parental Mr. and Mrs. Clabe Wilson home for the past several months.

Mrs. Alvin Scar and son Richard of Earlham came Saturday for a several-day visit at the parental Clabe Wilson home.

Curtis Field, Brady, Texas
August 1944
Junior

Dear Mom and Dad,

Doris and Warren stopped by on their way back to Marfa. I was playing basketball when they came, so I was all sweaty. I had to shake hands.

Joy sure does look like Doris. She smiled for me. I sure wish they could have stayed more than fifteen minutes. It's not long to visit with each other, but that's the way it goes.

I'm glad to hear you are buying an acreage. Five acres at $2500 in the country like that is a good buy. And only one mile to walk to Perry! That's the best city in the U.S. What a good deal.

Here's some more money to do whatever you want with. Don't put it away for me. Use it to purchase the new place or fix it up.

I think the allies will have Germany all bottled up before Christmas. The Pacific war will take longer. I hope we get word from Dale soon.

Junior

A/C JUNIOR WILSON, CURTIS FIELD, BRADY, TEXAS,
SUMMER 1944

CHAPTER 13

Autumn 1944

Santa Rosa, California
Autumn, 1944
Danny

The base where Danny was ordered next was dispersed and camouflaged. The barracks were more than a mile from the flight line and were in a plum orchard with an old barn across the road. A farmhouse and other buildings and orchards sat between the two runways.

Dear Mom and Dad,

My base is completely camouflaged. I have to cut through a vineyard or an orchard if I want to get anywhere. But from the air, a guy would have a rough time spotting it. There is a navy field nearby with long, concrete-block runways. Those can be spotted almost from Frisco!

Get the July 31st issue of "Life Magazine." It shows all the standard fighters in color. I like the P-38 better every time I fly it. It's the biggest one-man fighter there is. It is probably the plane I'll fly in combat.

I wish I could be there to help you move. Be sure to get electricity and a water system installed as soon as you can. I think five acres is just the right size. You're working for yourself and your little place!

With the action in the Wewak area, I hope it isn't much longer that we'll get to know about Dale. The one thing I want most is that Dale is alive and will be rescued. I might end up down there in combat, and if I am, I'll do my best to get Dale out of there.

Danny

Danny

Dear Mom and Dad,

That was a swell letter you wrote, Dad! I can see you getting a run for that Thompson hill with that corn. Must have taken plenty of shoveling. After this war, I'll make a damn good shoveler and truck driver after flying this 38.

The new place looks like it can be fixed up to look very modern with a white picket fence and all. Just a little paint, a few chickens, a couple of four o'clocks in the front yard, and a rusty pump, cow, and corn patch in the back.

I've completed my required training. I'm qualified as a twin and single engine fighter pilot. We'll start processing out soon. The army knows more about their men than the men do! I spent the day getting clearances and packing my duds. I'm taking only what is necessary.

Danny

FIRST HOUSE OWNED BY CLABE AND LEORA, ONE MILE
SOUTH OF PERRY, TAKEN JULY 1944

Danny got orders to leave by rail. Forbidden to tell his destination, he wrote that he would let the "censor get some exercise" and included that he was headed to the east coast for overseas embarkation.

He received letters from his parents, Junior, Doris, and a girl named Betty. All of his family wished him luck and best wishes, Junior told him to "give 'em hell," and Betty responded to a "swell letter" she had received from him.

Dear Danny,

I know it doesn't do any good to say take care of yourself, but I hope you do. You know those P-38s look pretty powerful and real exciting. I'd love to be flying with you and I know you're a good pilot. With 400 hours in the air, you ought to be.

Anyway, I'll always remember the fun we had at Balboa, and am sorry we didn't meet sooner. But then, that's the way things are. So be good and take care of yourself and be sure to let me know how your destination turns out.

Love,
Betty

Dallas County, Iowa
September 1944
Clabe and Leora

Clabe and Leora were busy working on the Minburn farm while preparing the new place. Every day they checked the mail for letters from their boys. Leora spent time writing to all of their children, sometimes six to ten letters a week. She kept everyone up to date on fixing up the new place, moving, the election, and hoping that the war would be over and everyone back home soon.

CLABE AND ONE OF HIS BIGGEST CHANNEL CATFISH

Dear Danny,

Dad tore out some of the old fence today. We painted and fixed up some in the house. Dad will repair the chicken house and build some fence before the ground freezes. We are beginning to love our new home more all the time. For six rooms and a path leading to the outhouse, I think we got a real bargain, and it was all made possible by you wonderful boys. We even paid off the car and have $258 left in the bank. We hope to have a phone put in by the end of the week.

I think we have the best bunch of boys and girls there ever was. We've had several others tell us so, too. I know it's true.

We've heard some good news from the Pacific. Carrier-based planes have gotten over 400 Japanese planes and some of their ships. I think Donald is right out there and wonder if you might be, too. Maybe you can give us some hints in your next letter.

Take good care of yourself, Danny. What a lot of things you boys will have to talk about when you all get home. We are so anxious to hear from you.

Love and luck to you,
Mom

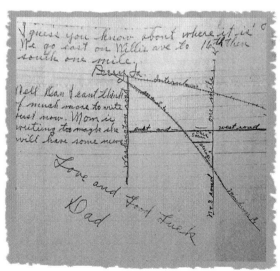

CLABE'S SKETCH OF WHERE THEIR ACREAGE WAS
LOCATED SOUTH OF PERRY, IOWA

Somewhere in Italy
Fall, 1944
Danny

Dear Mom and Dad,

I got myself a good tan while out to sea. My bunk was in a small compartment, so I spent a lot of time on the deck with my shirt off. The time went by pretty fast just watching the waves, sharks, and flying fish and listening to a phonograph that someone scraped up. When I saw seagulls and other odd-looking birds, I knew we were getting close to land.

No, Mom. I didn't go near where Don was. I'm now somewhere in Italy. Conditions are about as good as can be expected. Much better than the locals. People in the States can't realize how lucky they are unless they see a meager place like this. I'm living in a tent with four other pilots. It's rainy, cold, and the tent leaks. We are trying to scrape up materials to slap together a stone hut. I'll have to send you a picture of our accomplishment if it's accomplished. Ha!

It is pretty keen to be flying the P-38 again, but the steel-matted runways are really slick in wet weather. Muddy water makes a big spray each time we take off and land.

I can say that I've visited Naples, but not while I was here. I saw the hole in the Post Office made by a German time bomb which you probably remember reading about a year or so ago.

I got a letter and a V-mail from you folks, two letters from Doris, and one from Junior. It was like a field day! I would have liked to help you tear out the old fences at the new place. I heard it was near-zero weather back there in good old Iowa.

Have a look at pages 37-38 in the October 16th issue of "Life" magazine. I can't tell you where my base is, but this magazine has published a map with planes from the 15th Air Force heading north from bases near Foggia. Seems to put it right on the money if you know what I mean.

I hope we would hear from or about Dale soon. It would be the best morale boost all of us could have if we hear from him and know he is okay.

This letter will probably get to you after your birthday, Mom. I just want to let you know that I'm thinking of you always, for you to take care of yourself, and I give you all my love.

Danny

A/C JUNIOR WILSON, DALLAS, TEXAS

Perry Acreage
December 1944

Leora

Dear Danny,

A letter from you arrived right on my birthday! It sure was swell.

It's been a year since Dale's plane has been shot down. A long year, at that. If we could just hear that he is all right. A radio report said there might be an exchange of prisoners. It sure would be grand if Japan would do that and our Dale boy would be one of them freed. We are sure hoping and praying to get him back soon.

A box arrived from the Effects Bureau that had some of Dale's clothes and papers. If we could only get direct word from Dale, it would be the happiest Christmas for all of us.

I hope you had turkey and all the cranberry sauce you could eat for Thanksgiving. We heard all the boys in the service had turkey.

Our landlord stopped by the day before Thanksgiving and paid us. He told us to pick out a hog to butcher and said we deserved it for staying until the hard work was done. He told us we have the finest family of sons and daughters. Of course, we agree.

We sure will enjoy the new house better once all of you are back home. My greatest Christmas wish is for this war to be over.

Love,
Mom

Dear Danny,

Hurray! I got two letters from you today. They must have both been on a plane ride together part of the way. How wonderful to get letters from you.

Our chickens are doing fine. 103 pullets laid 75 eggs today. Dad put cornstalks around the hen house and banked snow against it on the north and west sides. The hens sing and are content.

It is so fun to have Richard around. He mocks things on the radio. He's a real energetic boy full of pep.

The Plymouth is still running fine and looks like new. We could probably sell it for a good price and bank the money, or maybe get a pickup, but it would be hard to find one. I think we will just keep the car until you boys come home and let you decide. I expect you boys will want a plane instead!

We don't have a phone yet. They are pretty scarce and there's several people ahead of us.

All our love and luck to you.
Mom

Dear Danny,

Richard is all excited about his Christmas tree we put up on Saturday night! He talks about Santa Claus all the time. I hope you have a good Christmas dinner and receive lots of mail. All I want for Christmas is word from my brother, Dale. I think that's the prayer of all of us. Next year we'll spend Christmas together and we'll really make up for lost time.

Love,
Darlene

Italy
December 1944
Danny

Dear Mom and Dad,

I just got two letters from home, a card with a picture of Richard from Darlene, and letters from Delbert, Junior, and Donald. I like all the little items that make up parts of your letters. I like to hear what you and Dad are doing at home.

I've been on more missions, one earlier today. Since they were bomber escort missions, they are longer. You've probably read or heard of certain missions over enemy territory or Germany proper.

We finished our stone shack. It has a brick floor, stove, running water and an electric light.

Yes, Mom, we had plenty of turkey and cranberries for Thanksgiving. It was plenty okay.

Can you send some film? I don't have a camera, but some other men do. It's just hard to get film.

Love,
Danny

THE PILOTS BUILT A STONE SHACK AT TRIOLO FIELD, ITALY. DECEMBER 1944

Italy
December 1944
Danny

Danny was with the 14th Fighter Group, 37th Fighter Squadron, part of the 15th Air Force based at Triolo, Italy.

LT. DANIEL WILSON, 15TH AIR FORCE,
15TH FIGHTER GROUP, 37TH FIGHTER SQUADRON

Dear Folks,

Yesterday I got to fly on my first combat mission over enemy territory. It was the longest flight I've ever taken in a P-38.

I got a pass to Rome for four days over Christmas. We rode along in an open-air Jeep and drove past many flattened towns on our way. We got to stay in a hotel while we were in Rome. It was a lot cleaner than other towns. We had good chow and a dance every night. People are well-dressed and the stores are full of things, but most of it is expensive. We had a tour of St. Paul's Church, the Coliseum, and the Catacombs.

On Christmas Eve, we attended a midnight mass at St. Peter's Church in the Vatican City. The place was huge and beautiful. Pope Pius XII was going to be there, so we figured we would get to see him. Quite a number of other people had the same idea. We found ourselves in a predicament we wished we weren't in. It was actually fascinating to see what people will try to get by with in a crowd. We did get to see the pope.

Later at the hotel, there was a Christmas party for orphan kids. They got some presents and were more fortunate than the kids living among the ruins of their bombed towns.

I expect this letter will be received by you a few days after your birthday, Dad. I want to let you know that I am thinking of you and Mom always.

Danny

DAN WILSON WITH HIS P-38

DAN WILSON WITH HIS
P-38 LIGHTNING, TRIOLO FIELD, ITALY.
SHOWS THE STEEL MARSTON
MAT USED FOR RUNWAYS

Greenville, Texas
Late, 1944
Junior

Dear Mom and Dad,

I soloed in the BT-13. This plane makes more noise than any other. I like a lot of noise.

There's a lot of good food here at Basic. Lots of greens, fruit, and milk. I have a pint of milk at every meal, and even some 100% bran for breakfast once in a while. I also keep busy working out with some barbells.

How is the new place coming? I sure wish I could come home and get a good hunting trip in. Hopefully in February. A hind leg of a young squirrel would taste like ice cream compared to some of the Army chow I've eaten.

You may have read this in the newspaper, but the whole cadet program is being delayed five weeks. All the way from Pre-flight to Advanced. There isn't as much demand for pilots anymore.

The Post Commander promised we would get some flying in an Advanced trainer, so it won't be so bad after all. I'll have over a hundred hours of Basic and will be a better pilot with more ground school and flying.

I hope to be graduating in April. Maybe I'll be home to help put the garden in this spring.

Try not to worry and work too hard.

Junior

Waco, Texas
Late 1944
Junior

Dear Mom and Dad,

I suppose you are having cool weather up there now. Probably some good coon-hunting weather. We had a pet coon on a long chain here at the base. We could pet him like a kitten. I don't think I'll kill any more of them.

I'm in Waco for more Basic Training. The gym is right across the road. They have brand new barbells. By Christmas, I'll be in Advanced Training in fighters. They want the younger boys in the fighters since they can stand more strain and their reflexes are faster.

Are you having fun fixing up your new home? I'm sending home more money. Maybe it will help buy a bucket of coal or a big box of bran from the Thriftway.

Junior

Dear Doris,

I'm gonna have to get a more powerful name than Junior pretty soon. I don't look like a Junior any more. Getting kind of big.

Junior

Doris

Dear Junior,

I hope your training time will be extended so the war will be over and you don't have to get in on it all. I suppose you have other ideas about it. Maybe next Christmas we will all be home. I sure hope so. That would be the best Christmas ever.

Doris

Perry Acreage
December 1944

Leora

Junior did get home for Christmas that year. He was the first son to see the "Wilson Ranch." Leora spent Christmas Day writing letters.

Dear Danny,

It's clear and cold here at home. Junior came yesterday about 10:30 a.m. He came walking in from Perry. He gave us hints in his letter we received on Friday that he might get to come, so we looked for him at the train on Saturday night. Junior sure looks good. We are having a good visit. It's going to be too short.

It will be wonderful when all you boys are home together. I can just imagine all of you telling your stories of your experiences. We will enjoy listening.

Mom

Junior

Junior also wrote to Danny before catching the train in Des Moines.

Dear Danny,

The folks are looking good. The ranch is a pretty nice little place. It's got good soil and a pretty good house. They are keeping me well fed here.

Junior

Clabe and Leora took their youngest son to catch the train for Texas on a bright, moonlit night. The moon was so bright, the snow sparkled.

They were both lonesome after Junior left, the same way when any of them came home and then had to leave for someplace far away. They were glad to stay busy and keep their minds occupied. Otherwise, they worried.

They worried about Donald in combat in the Pacific, about Danny in combat in Europe, and about Dale, wherever he was.

CHAPTER 14

Early 1945

Italy
January 1945
Danny

Dear Mom and Dad,

Heavy snow fell here on New Year's Eve. To bring in the new year, all of the airmen put up a small barrage outside with our .45s. On New Year's Day I went on a hike with one of my shack-mates. It was okay to walk around in the snow, even if it wasn't back in Iowa where there is a little game to go along with it.

Two of the pilots in my hut are from Iowa, the other from Oklahoma. The Okie can't make out worth hell in arguments in this hut. Ha! They all are a bunch of damn swell buddies. We definitely have the best-looking hut in the squadron.

I sure enjoyed seeing pictures of your new place. It sure looks keen. It's the best land, in the best state, in the best damn country in the world. That's for damn sure.

You probably got my letter saying that I was in Rome a while back. I've also been to Naples and Foggia, but not in the same way.

The weather is hindering combat missions. During bad weather we have classes and practice in the Link trainer.

I can't think of anything new to write about that would pass the censor's scrutiny.

Danny

Perry Acreage
January 1945

Leora

Clabe and Leora were alone on New Year's Day. Clabe spent the day oiling the boys' guns. Once in a while, he'd go out to get a rabbit so it wouldn't eat their garden that summer.

A picture from Doris of baby Joy arrived. Leora framed it to match the ones of Richard and Leora Darlene, arranging all three on the big console radio.

Leora

Dear Danny,

You children's letters are Dad's and my brightest time of day—mail time with letters!

We heard some big news from the Philippines. They are doing good so far and I hope that continues. We know Donald is right there close.

It was exciting to hear that you got to see such wonderful things in Rome over Christmas. All the work and masterpieces of the ages.

Darlene, Sam, and Richard are here to celebrate your dad's birthday. Richard notices every detail. I think he will become a good scholar someday.

I'm sending some pictures from when Junior was home. He said our little Dallas County place was worth about the whole state of Texas.

Love and best of luck to you always. And God bless you.

Mom

Clabe

Dear Danny,

Mom and I have got about all the winter we want already. I'm anxious to set out some trees and get things fixed up. I plan to seed the place down with alfalfa this spring and get a cow or two. Your mom is getting ready to order her baby chicks. That is the kind of work she likes.

I picked some corn with a sled and husked it by hand. Besides writing letters, your mom does all the washing and hangs the clothes up here in the house. She cleans the chicken house and sometimes helps me pick corn.

Take care of yourself.
Dad

Marfa, Texas
January 1945
Doris

Knowing how it had encouraged their folks, Doris was glad to hear that Junior had gotten home. "I even feel better!" she wrote to her folks.

While Warren was on a cross-country flight at night, Doris wrote letters home, to Donald, and answered a letter from Danny. "We pray to God you are lucky and are back home to stay before long," she wrote. "We don't want any heroes in the family—just all of us home."

Doris wrote home saying how she hoped Danny would get his required missions done so he could come home and be an instructor.

"But here is the big disappointment around here—no toofs yet!" she wrote. "Is there such a thing about a baby having no teeth?"

New London, Connecticut
January 1945
Delbert and Evelyn

Delbert and Evelyn each took a turn writing in a letter home. Del was now at the Submarine School at New London. He wrote about playing "peek-a-boo" with baby Leora. "Sure wish everyone could be as lucky and happy as I am."

Evelyn wrote that baby Leora didn't have any teeth either. "I'm sure glad you told me Joy doesn't have any teeth yet. I was getting worried. The baby next door had teeth when it was only two months old!"

Perry Acreage
January 1945
Clabe and Leora

The Wilsons were encouraged when a letter from the Army Air Forces Headquarters arrived stating it was now permissible to release the names of the crew members who were with Dale when he was lost. Addresses of the families were included.

They received letters from families of Dale's crew. All of the letters said about the same thing—the crew was on a strafing mission about 50 feet above ground, the plane was hit by enemy fire, then hit the water, rose again, and then settled into the water. All information pointed to the idea that the crew would have

SGT. WILLIE TED SHARPTON, LOST ON HIS FIRST MISSION ON THE B-25 CREW LOST IN NEW GUINEA

had plenty of time to get out of the plane and get to land, but were likely prisoners of war.

One of the letters came from Essie Sharpton, the mother of S/Sgt. Willie Ted Sharpton, a member of the same crew as Dale.

Dear Mr. and Mrs. Wilson,

This was my son's first mission. They usually just use five boys as a crew, but that morning they put six in—two at the big gun, one to load, and one to shoot. My son was called to make this extra man.

Nine planes were in formation and our boys were in the tail plane. They flew over Wewak, dropped their bombs, then flew out over the air strip on Cape Boram. They were 50–75 feet over the airfield strafing when the plane was hit. Someone in the lead plane said it looked like a rudder post was knocked out of the tail. The plane hit water, rose a bit, then hit and settled. It seemed as if the controls were jammed.

The airman in the same mission that I talked to said he has seen the same thing happen since, even a plane that had been shot up worse, and the crew was saved. He expected that they'd gotten out, as they were near enough to the shore to swim there and were prisoners of the Japanese.

So, we'll keep on praying, hoping, and waiting. Someday we'll know more. In the meantime, we'll trust God to care for them.

Essie Sharpton

Perry Acreage
February 1945
Clabe and Leora

Clabe and Leora finally got Danny's hint about Foggia, Italy, and found it on a map.

Darlene and Sam tried to visit them often, usually on Sundays. Richard kept them entertained with little songs and Mother Goose rhymes.

They hadn't heard from Donald in about three weeks, so were aware he was probably in the thickest of war in the Pacific.

Names were being announced over the radio of the 510 POWs liberated on Luzon, several from Iowa. How they wished that Dale would be one of them. "Our day for that joy is coming," Leora hoped and prayed.

When one of the families of a man on Dale's crew received their son's things from the Effects Bureau, they found a picture of the crew with their plane. It was taken in November 1943—the same month they were shot down. The names of the boys were all listed on the back. Mr. Stack, the father of another missing crew member, enlarged the picture and sent it to each of the families. "Dale looks so natural with his sleeves rolled up, collar open, and a cap on," Leora quipped.

Liberation of prisoners continued. "Manila is ours!" Leora shouted when she heard the news. "We may get word that Dale and a lot more are liberated before long. That time is coming!"

The Wilsons were encouraged by the news from the Philippines, but they didn't think Dale was there or they would have heard something. "He may have better treatment where he is than if he'd been in a Manila prison. I think their meanest Japs were in the Philippines. Of course we know there are some Japs who are humane."

The news from both Europe and the Pacific was encouraging. Leora noticed a map of Europe in the newspaper showing the routes of planes, including one to Vienna. She knew that Danny might be in that formation, or a similar one, and hoped that the war would be over by the time her next letter got to him.

BACK: LT. WIELAND, LT. WILSON, LT. STACK. FRONT: SSGT. WOOLLEN-WEBER, SGT. BANKO, THE NEXT MAN WASN'T ON THE CREW WHEN THE BOMBER WAS SHOT DOWN.

Dear Danny,

We have our minds and prayers all over the globe for our very own boys, and of course, for others too. We heard that Tokyo has taken a bombing. We bet they wished they had never heard of Pearl Harbor. Tokyo is just getting the beginning of what they are in for.

We hope to hear soon about Dale being freed and that he might just come walking in one day. It would be the grandest. We would get busy sending cables and telegrams to everyone with the wonderful news.

Your dad is eager for weather good enough to work outdoors. A neighbor stopped by and asked if he would help him that spring and summer. Farmers really need help around here.

Hope to see you soon, Danny boy.

Love,
Mom

Italy
February 1945
Danny

Dear Mom and Dad,

I've heard from everyone else, but not from Donald for some time. He's without a doubt the one in the family who's seeing the most action.

It's good that all of you parents from Dale's crew can correspond with each other. I'm sure Dale will be walking in through the door sometime soon.

Danny

PILOTS LT. WILSON AND
LT. TURNBULL

LT. HARRY WOLD, DANNY
WILSON'S BEST FRIEND

Mesa, Arizona
February 1945
Doris

Doris received a book-length letter from her mother with information from parents of Dale's crew. Her mom also sent photos of Junior when he was home.

Warren was getting a cross-country flight home for seven days. He hoped to get to visit the Wilsons in person and tell them all about eight-month-old Joy firsthand.

While Warren was in Iowa, Doris learned that he was to be transferred to Williams Field in Arizona, so he hurried back to Marfa. Doris had everything packed, and anything that wouldn't fit in the car was ready to ship back to Iowa.

Dear Mom and Dad,

We shipped seven boxes, two army trunks, and two pasteboard boxes back home. I know it's an awful lot to shove off on you. When we left Marfa, the Chevy was loaded till it looked like a rowboat. I didn't want to leave things behind, especially if Warren gets sent across. If he does, every little trinket will be priceless to me.

Oh! I haven't told you yet...guess who has a tooth peepin' through!"

Love,
Doris

Victoria, Texas
Winter 1945

Junior

Dear Folks,

I just saw the movie "Winged Victory." If it ever comes to Perry, you should see it. It gives a pretty good picture of what cadet life is like, considerably glorified, of course. You'll see the ol' BT-13 in the night flying, like I flew at Majors Field and all. Of course, there's the story of a married cadet and a bomber pilot—to satisfy the emotional people I suppose.

We can tune in to WHO Radio from Des Moines here in the barracks. It sounds pretty good.

Don't work too hard.

Junior

Dear Dunny,

I saw some newsreel showing lousy weather and hardships for the Fifteenth Air Force in Italy. I guess you're in the middle of all of that.

A captain from the 15th who was in the raids on the Balkans and Munich came and talked to us about the war. He sure does appreciate the bomber crews and the boys in the P-38s.

I'm up to 180 pounds. If I get any heavier, I'll end up as a co-pilot on a flyin' boxcar yet!

Junior

Junior sent the following announcement home:

The Aloe Army Air Field of Victoria, Texas announced the graduation of Class 45A on Sunday morning, March eleventh, nineteen-hundred and forty-five, Post Theatre. Claiborne J. Wilson, Flight Officer, Air Corps, Army of the United States.

It will make another pair of wings on your coat, Mom!

Junior

CHAPTER 15

Spring 1945

Perry Acreage, Iowa
Spring 1945
Leora

Dear Son Danny,

Hope this finds you doing alright and in your usual good health. I suppose it looks like spring in Italy by the time you receive this. I hope you'll get to hear your favorite meadowlarks.

Junior is to graduate and get his wings on March 11th. We hope he'll get a furlough home. We'll be watching for him just in case.

Your dad is in the workshop in the barn. We plan to move the brooder house in time for my baby chicks to arrive.

Lots of love and luck to you.
Mom

A telegram arrived at the Wilson's home on March 10, 1945:

WASHINGTON DC VIA MINBURN IOWA CLABE D WILSON MAR 10 THE SECRETARY OF WAR DESIRES ME TO EXPRESS HIS DEEP REGRET THAT YOUR SON SECOND LIEUTENANT DANIEL S WILSON HAS BEEN REPORTED MISSING IN ACTION SINCE NINETEENTH FEBRUARY OVER AUSTRIA IF FURTHER DETAILS OR OTHER INFORMATION ARE RECEIVED YOU WILL BE PROMPTLY NOTIFIED J A ULIO THE ADJUTANT GENERAL

Dear Mrs. Wilson,

I am certain that the news that your son, Second Lieutenant Daniel S. Wilson, is missing in action must have been a great shock to you, and that you have been eagerly awaiting further data. Although I can give you no definite information as to Daniel's fate, the following facts may be of some help.

On February 19, 1945, your son took his P-38 on a mission to escort a formation of bombers to Bruck, Austria. After reaching the target, the fighter escort set out to destroy enemy communications in the vicinity of Graz, Austria. When the flight reassembled after attacking a train, Daniel was missing. Two planes returned to the area but could find no trace of your son or his plane. Should there be a change in his status at any time in the future, you will be notified immediately by the War Department.

Daniel's personal possessions have been carefully packed for shipment to the Effects Quartermaster, Army Effects Bureau, Kansas City, Missouri, who will forward them to the designated beneficiary.

For the courageous manner in which he carried out his hazardous duties during the course of frequent combat operations, your son has been awarded the Air Medal with Oak Leaf Cluster. I share pride in his achievements and your hopes for his safe return.

Sincerely,
Major General Twining, Commanding General of the Fifteenth Air Force

Leora continued to write to Danny, holding on to the hope that he would be found and rescued.

Dear Son Danny,

We are so anxious to hear from you, that you are well and alright. We hope and pray for your safety day and night. Hope to get good word from you soon.
Love,
Mom

Junior was able to get a furlough after earning his wings. Just as his brothers had done, he had his picture taken at Edmonson's in Perry.

F/O C. JUNIOR WILSON, PERRY, IOWA, MARCH 1945

It was hard for Junior to celebrate with two of his brothers missing in action. While home, he spent an entire day hiking. He saw jack rabbits, cottontails, and snakes. He had taken his rifle but didn't use it.

Junior caught a train in Des Moines bound for Waco, Texas.

CLABE AND LEORA WILSON WITH THEIR 1942
PLYMOUTH, PERRY, MARCH 1945

Dear Mr. and Mrs. Wilson,

I wanted to update you on additional information that we have received regarding your son, Daniel S. Wilson.

Lieutenant Wilson was the pilot of a P-38 fighter plane which departed from Italy on an escort and bombing mission to Vienna, Austria on 19 February 1945. The report reveals that during this mission near Bruck, Austria, after bombing an enemy train, your son was observed to drop back to take pictures of the damage. His fighter was neither seen nor contacted by radio after that time. Pilots of accompanying planes circled over the area several times, but no trace of the plane was found. It is regretted that we are unable to furnish any other details concerning the disappearance of Lieutenant Wilson.

We are actively continuing to search for missing personnel. As our armies advance over enemy occupied territory, special troops are assigned to this task. Additionally, allies frequently send us details to aid us with information. We are relying on this information in your son's case.

Sincerely,
Major N.W. Reed, Acting Chief of the Air Corps Notification Branch
Headquarters, Army Air Forces

April in Perry, Iowa brought a spring blizzard. Two hundred White Rock and 174 Barred Rock chicks arrived fine in spite of the storm. Leora checked on her chicks a couple of times each night. She and Clabe were also busy planting potatoes, lettuce, peas, onions, flowers, and setting out grapes, rose bushes, shrubs, rhubarb, strawberries, and sowing grass.

The work had to be done, but it did not erase the worry over Dale and Danny, both missing in action.

New London, Connecticut
March 1945
Delbert and Evelyn

Dear Mom and Dad,

It seems to me you have had more than your share of bad news. Even though I haven't met any of you yet, those boys are as dear to me as my own brothers.

Delbert had another horrible dream. He woke me crying in his sleep. I don't know how he is going to handle all of this.

Thank you for the pictures of Danny. I was reading your letter to little Leora and when she heard her name out loud, she laughed and jabbered as if she knew what I was reading. Del can't get over all that she does.

We think the war in Germany will be over soon and more prisoners will be rescued in the Pacific. We hope and pray to God that everyone will be home soon and to stay. What a day that will be! I have so many nice, new relatives I haven't met yet.

I hope and pray that Danny and Dale are safe with friends.

Chins up and God bless you both.
Evelyn

Dear Mom and Dad,

Evelyn just told me the news about Danny. I just can't even describe how I feel. I guess it's no use trying to—we all probably feel the same way. At times, I feel like a heel being on this soft job here in the States with those kids out there.

I figure Dan might have bailed out of his plane. Most fliers over there do. Austria has some pretty rugged country and a plane that lands at 110 MPH can't be put down in a hay field. He might have gotten as far as the Russian lines. If that's the case, we should get word of him soon.

I can't take my eyes off the pictures you sent of Danny—he looks like a determined fighter pilot. Do you have the names of the other boys in the stone hut? I'd like to write to them.

Mom, you just keep Dad from worryin' and frettin' so much. I don't want him overworking or straining to help other farmers.

Delbert

San Antonio, Texas
March 1945
Junior

When Junior arrived in Waco, his shipping orders were waiting. Three others had the same orders, and all went together to Randolph Field, San Antonio. Junior thought it was the prettiest field he had been on yet.

Dear Mom and Dad,

I hope we get some good news from Dan soon. I sent my graduation announcement to him, but it was returned. I heard that the U.S. forces and Russians have met and cut Germany in two. Austria must be in Allied hands by now. They'll get Danny out of there.

I got a letter from Donald. He's still pounding the Japs. I hope he comes back and stays back. He's seen enough action.

How's everything going on the ranch? I suppose the corn planters are clicking all over the land. Don't work too hard at the neighbor's, Dad. You're independent on the little ranch, so take the highest bidder! Ha!

Love,
Junior

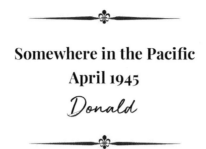

Somewhere in the Pacific
April 1945
Donald

Dear Mom and Dad,

I just couldn't answer your letter right away. The news of Danny came as a shock. I hadn't heard from him for about a month, so I wondered if something was wrong. I feel like I am just about immune to anything, anymore.

The news from out this way is a pretty good key as to where I might be. I believe the Navy should take fifty percent of the credit for retaking the Philippines.

I hope you folks hear something about Danny and Dale soon. Keep me posted on Darlene and Sam—I predict they will have another boy.

Donald

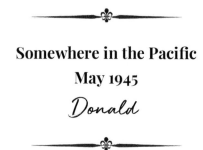

Somewhere in the Pacific
May 1945
Donald

Dear Mom and Dad,

I'm glad that Germany has finally surrendered, but I hope people don't think the war is over just yet. I figure the war in the Pacific will last another two years. It looks like I'll be in the Pacific for the duration, but I hope some electrician who wonders what it is all about will come relieve me for a while. I'm getting some rest, but it's a strain. I'm okay as long as I keep busy, but after this war I'm gonna need about six months in the woods.

The latest good news is that the Australians have captured Wewak. We might be getting news about Dale before long. I sure hope he's okay and not starved. We'll keep hoping for the best.

I'm sending you folks a list of my past combat operations. It might be a good souvenir to show years later for someone who wants to know what I did during the war.

Donald

Donald also sent some pictures home to Rose. Afraid they may get ruined, he wanted to make sure to keep them safe. "I lost a bunch of good pictures, once," Donald told her, referring to the sinking of the *Yorktown*.

Perry Acreage
May 1945

Leora and Clabe

All the men in Warren's class who had over 500 hours were given one day to get to Yuma, Arizona. They wanted all the men who might fly B-29s to get another 400 hours of flight time in a four-engine plane.

Yuma was even smaller that Marfa, and there were no places for families to live. Doris and Joy returned to Iowa to stay at the Perry acreage.

On May 2, Darlene and Sam had another baby boy, Robert Edward, six days before Germany surrendered to the Allies. While Darlene and baby were in the hospital, Richard stayed with his grandparents along with Aunt Doris and cousin Joy.

Mr. and Mrs. Claiborne Wilson,

It has been my fervent hope that favorable information would be forthcoming so that you might be relieved from the great anxiety which you have borne during these months. It is therefore with deep regret that I must state that no further report in your son, Daniel's case has been forwarded to the War Department.

I assure you we are making every effort to establish what happened to anyone and everyone reported missing or missing in action. We will contact you if we receive additional information or in three months.

Major General Ulio

Mr. and Mrs. Wilson,

Enclosed is a check for $18.76 which represents the amount of funds belonging to Daniel Wilson at the time he was reported missing in action. The Army Effects Bureau has not received any other property belonging to him. Keep the money safe for the owner, pending his return. In the event that he is later reported a casualty, the funds should be distributed according to the laws of the state of his legal residence. I sincerely hope that such distribution will not be necessary.

Kansas City Quartermaster Depot

CHAPTER 16

Summer 1945

Perry, Iowa
July 1945
From: The Perry Daily Chief

Donald Wilson Serves on Famed Hancock

Aboard the aircraft carrier U.S.S. Hancock in the Western Pacific, Donald Wilson, chief electrician's mate, U.S.N., son of Mr. and Mrs. C.D. Wilson, Route 2, Perry, Iowa, shared this carrier's unequaled one-day record of 71 enemy aircraft shot down, 19 probably downed, 8 destroyed, and 12 damaged on the ground, during a raid over the Tokyo area on Feb. [16], 1945.

Before this performance, the U.S.S. Hancock gained fame by bombarding Okinawa for eight straight days, during which the record of 600 individual plane strikes was set. The result was 10 ships sunk, including three attack transports, a sub tender, and a large tanker, with 22 Japanese aircraft and industrial and chemical plants destroyed.

Commissioned a little more than a year ago, the carrier took part in operations off Samar, supported the Leyte invasion, attacked shipping in the South China Sea, and provided air support for the Iwo Jima campaign.

In 190 strikes by the Hancock, she accounted for nine warships, 32 merchant ships, 241 enemy planes, and an indefinite number of aircraft destroyed on the ground.

Each crewman has eight solid pages of battle actions and commendations entered in his service record.

Wilson, who is 28, has been in the Navy since 1934 and served aboard the carrier Yorktown until she was sunk. His last visit home was in June of 1943.

Wilson has four brothers also in service—Delbert is an electrician's mate first class in the Navy; Dale and Danny are second lieutenants in the Army Air Force; and Junior is a flight officer in the Air Corps.

A brother-in-law, Lt. Warren D. Neal, is taking B-29 training.

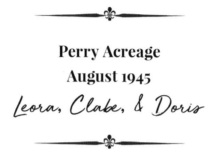

Perry Acreage
August 1945
Leora, Clabe, & Doris

August 6 brought the shocking news that, after weeks of firebombing Japanese cities, the United States had dropped an atomic bomb on the city of Hiroshima, Japan.

The world news also started to hold some hope, bringing an expectant feeling in the Wilson home. On August 8, Russia entered the war against Japan. Americans believed the war would be over soon. Clabe and Leora held on to hope that they would receive word from Danny and Dale.

The next day a second atomic bomb was dropped on Japan, this time on the city of Nagasaki.

The Wilsons' mail had already been delivered, but later that day their mailman, Oscar Daniels, returned and knocked on the door.

The movies always depicted this kind of moment with two men in uniform coming to the door to deliver a telegram with the dreaded news. In rural Iowa, this was delivered by your own mailman. Clabe and Leora expected confirmation of Danny's death. They retreated to their bedroom in tears while Doris went to the door.

She opened the envelope as the words in front of her began to swim.

ALOEFIELD VICTORIA TEX AUG 9 MRS. LEORA FRANCES WILSON RTE 2 PERRY IOWA: I DEEPLY REGRET TO INFORM YOU OF THE DEATH OF YOUR SON FLIGHT OFFICER CLAIBORNE JUNIOR WILSON AS A RESULT OF AIRPLANE ACCIDENT THIS MORNING. PLEASE ADVISE FUNERAL DIRECTOR WHO WILL HANDLE INTERMENT ARRANGEMENTS AND NAME AND ADDRESS OF PERSON WHO WILL INCUR AND BE RESPONSIBLE FOR INTERMENT EXPENSES. REMAINS WILL BE SHIPPED TO ANY PLACE DESIGNATED BY YOU AT GOVERNMENT EXPENSE. ESCORT WILL BE SENT IF DESIRED. PLEASE REPLY BY WESTERN UNION COLLECT. STOYTE O ROSS COLONEL AIR CORPS COMMANDING OFFICER.

The telegram didn't say Danny. It said "Junior."

But Junior was safe in Texas. It couldn't be Junior.

In tears, Doris reluctantly showed the unbelievable news to her folks. They wept together. After several minutes, Mr. Daniels knocked on the door. "Is there anything I can do for you folks?"

The Wilsons were still on a waiting list for a phone, so Doris drove into Perry to make phone calls and send telegrams.

Perry, Iowa

August 1945

The Wilson Acreage

Another telegram arrived soon after with more news about Junior:

ALOE FIELD VICTORIA TEXAS MRS LEORA FRANCES
WILSON RT 2 PERRY IOWA

REMAINS OF LATE FLIGHT OFFICER CLAIBORNE
JUNIOR WILSON HAVE BEEN PREPARED AND ARE BEING
SHIPPED AT GOVERNMENT EXPENSE ACCOMPANIED
BY MILITARY ESCORT LT RALPH T WOODS DUE TO
ARRIVE IN PERRY IOWA ON CHICAGO MILWAUKEE ST
PAUL AND PACIFIC RAILROAD AT 1153 PM ON 11 AUGUST
THE GOVERNMENT WILL PAY TO PERSON INCURRING
INTERMENT EXPENSES A SUM NOT IN EXCESS OF FIFTY
DOLLARS CERTIFICATE TO BE FILLED OUT FOR
INTERMENT EXPENSES FOLLOWS ROSS CO AAFLD

At Aloe Field, Lt. Ralph Woods received a message from the chap-
lain asking if he would accompany Junior's casket home to Iowa. He
was nervous and sad, but honored to be chosen. He and Junior had
bunked together, played basketball, and shared stories about their
families.

Delbert would arrive at 4:30 the next morning. The Wilson house was so tiny, Doris and her toddler slept in a closet so Ralph Woods and Delbert could share the extra bed.

Violet Hill Cemetery
Perry, Iowa
August 1945

It was a Monday. Sixteen hundred planes attacked Tokyo. There was still no word about surrendering.

Junior's funeral took place at 2:30 in the afternoon at the First Christian Church in Perry. The forty-eight-star flag from the casket was ceremoniously folded. Lieutenant Woods presented the grieving parents with this symbol of their son's service and sacrifice.

Claiborne Junior Wilson was the first in the family to be buried in Perry's Violet Hill Cemetery.

By Monday evening, President Truman announced that Japan had agreed to unconditional surrender.

The USS Hancock
August 1945
Donald

The Japanese had announced that they would not surrender unless they could keep their emperor.

Since his ship was still in combat, preparing for troop landings on Japan, Donald had not yet heard about Junior.

Dear Mom and Dad,

We expected this first actual peace feeler from the Japs to be rejected because it wouldn't be an unconditional surrender. The emperor of Japan is a war criminal, so we will accept nothing less than full surrender. This war will continue until we get the terms we want.

There's a chance Dale could be in Japan. None of the POW camps are marked, but the U.S. knows where some of them are.

The Japs operate on deceit and treachery. They can't be trusted. If they don't fully surrender, the whole island will be bombed. That's really taking a chance that Dale and the other POWs will come through okay. I'd sure hate to see kids Richard's age twenty years from now say we didn't do the job up right. If that's the case, then they'll have to go through this same hell. Possibly worse.

Donald

INTERIOR COMMUNICATIONS GANG, USS HANCOCK, AUGUST 1945,
BETWEEN THE JAPANESE SURRENDER AND OFFICIAL SIGNING
OF THE PAPERS. DONALD WILSON IS SEVENTH FROM LEFT.

Dear Mom and Dad,

The war came to an abrupt end, didn't it? I hope Dale comes out of one of those camps. Have you heard anything about Danny?

It's hard for me to believe that the war is really over. I'll have to stay on the Hancock and be on guard for a while just in case some of those Japs didn't get the word that they are whipped.

Have Warren and Junior left the U.S.? If so, they might both get in on the occupation of Japan.

Hoping for more good news,
Donald

Dear Mom and Dad,

I just got Doris' telegram about Junior. I suppose you've been waiting to hear from me. I've tried several times to write, but I'm just in such a shock. It's hard to believe.

I know Junior would not have been happy doing anything other than what he was doing. Such is life, I guess.

Donald

The Navy owed Donald thirty days' reenlistment leave plus thirty of rehabilitation. He requested a tour of shore duty. Rose expected him home soon, and they hoped to make a trip to Iowa.

Perry, Iowa
August 1945
Doris

Dear Warren,

It seems like a terrible dream and so long ago! It still doesn't seem possible. Sometimes I think that maybe it was someone else and not Junior at all. The casket couldn't be opened and not being able to see him makes it all even harder.

Ralph Woods, the lieutenant who escorted Junior home, told us what happened. They had all been in formation with P-40s and noticed a plane losing altitude. They had no radio connection. A short while later, they noticed flames coming from the plane. That was the last they saw of it. Junior's body was quite a ways away from the burned plane. There was an explosion in the plane before Junior was clear. He had already pulled the rip cord. We are all sure that Junior hated the thought of losing his plane, so he waited too long.

Promise me that if anything goes wrong with your plane you will jump quick! We don't care how many B-29s you abandon. They aren't worth a cent compared to your life.

I hope you will be out of the army soon so we can rest easy and be happy with our cute little family on our little farm.

Love,
Doris

Perry, Iowa
August 1945
Clabe, Leora, & Doris

Life, even while mourning, continued on day-by-day. On the Thursday following the funeral, Clabe and Leora dug nine baskets of potatoes and went to Grimes to look at cows. On Friday, they sold twenty-five roosters and Clabe did more painting on the barn.

Clabe, Leora, and Doris visited the cemetery every Sunday to put flowers on Junior's grave. It still didn't seem possible to any of them.

A couple of letters from Texas arrived at the Wilson home.

⚜

Dear Mr. and Mrs. Wilson,

My name is O.A. Stirl. I'm a farmer from Nordheim, Texas and I witnessed your son's plane crash. I felt it my duty to send you the information I have because of the supreme sacrifice your son has paid for his country.

Your son's plane was in a three-plane formation. One of them left a smoking trail. A flame appeared and the plane began to circle downward but seemed like it was under control. Between 500 and 1000 feet, a terrific explosion tore the plane apart.

The nose of the plane was buried nearly five feet in a cornfield and the rest of the plane was in flames. Help arrived in just a few minutes. I did not see a parachute, but I assumed that your son had bailed out in time until I learned of his death in the local paper.

Here is that clipping:

The Nordheim View: Army Plane Crashes at Tick City

"*Flight officer Claiborne J. Wilson, 20, of Perry, Iowa, was killed Thursday when his P-40 training plane crashed on a combat training flight 10 miles southwest of Yorktown, near Nordheim. The accident occurred at approximately 10:15.*

"*The son of Mr. and Mrs. C.D. Wilson of Perry, Iowa, Flight Officer Wilson graduated from Aloe Field in class 45-A.*

"*A board of officers have been appointed to determine the cause of the accident.*

"*Residents of Tick City, Nordheim residents, and Boy Scouts assisted Army officials from Aloe Field in the search for the body of the young flyer which fell about a hundred yards from the crash.*

"*Gus Pargmann found the body in a thicket not far from the crash.*"

Dear Mr. and Mrs. Wilson,

May we, a few of your son Claiborne's many friends, take this time to extend to you our deepest sympathy in your hour of sorrow.

We called him C.J. We ate our meals with him, played with him, and worked with him. We listened to him tell of life on the farm, of his family, and of his friends. To us, C.J. was one of the boys, a fine soldier, a fine pilot, and a fine friend.

Below are a few of our names. We hope in this way to convey to you a little of our individual appreciation for the things your son lived and died for.

His Buddies,

The letter from Aloe Field, Texas, was signed by eighteen men, including Ralph T. Woods, the young pilot who had accompanied Junior's casket from Texas to Iowa.

New London, Connecticut
August 1945
Delbert

Dear Mom and Dad,

I was granted a Special-Order Discharge and will be home soon. Two boxes are on their way to Iowa now. Get some help with them, Dad...they lift pretty hard. Make sure you open them, too. The heavy one has a carton of Luckies and one of Camels for me.

Sure miss Doris and Joy, too. We sure will be glad when our girls can get together. I hope Warren doesn't have to go over. I look for enough volunteer airmen to do the patrol.

Keep your chins up and try not to worry too much. Best of luck always.

Delbert

Perry, Iowa

The Air Corps Transportation Officer from Aloe AAF sent, in triplicate, a Government Bill of Lading along with a copy of a list of Personal Effects belonging to the Late Flight Officer Claiborne J. Wilson.

Clabe was to complete the Consignee's Certificate of Delivery on the Original Bill of Lading and surrender the same to the local delivering carrier to return the copies. Also enclosed was a money order representing cash and currency belonging to Junior.

Doris turned twenty-seven on August 30. Clabe watched Joy while Leora and Doris went into Perry to see the movie "State Fair."

Clabe finished painting the barn that weekend. They listened to the surrender broadcast over the radio from Tokyo on September 2, 1945.

The Wilsons were glad the war was over, but heartsick over the loss of one son and the two who were still missing.

CHAPTER 17

Autumn 1945

The Pacific
Autumn 1945
Donald

Using a local point system, Donald was at the top of the list for leave. He thought he'd make it back to the U.S. during the latter part of October or first of November.

Dear Mom and Dad,

It is still hard for me to realize that Junior is gone. So much good and bad has happened in the last few months, I'm kind of going in circles still. Even the peace seems odd to me.

I still have hope that Dale will come out of one of the POW camps, but most of them are in poor health. As soon as a camp is located, we get supplies and medical attention there right away. It sure looks to me that there is going to be a lot of work out here for our firing squads with all the reports on the treatment of our men.

Soon the censorship of mail will be lifted and I'll be able to write natural again. On both sides of the paper if I care to! Ha!

Donald

Aberdeen, Washington
Autumn 1945

Dear Mom and Dad,

Gee won't it be grand when they all come home again? I'm waiting on needles and pins hoping to hear something about Dan and Dale soon. Donald has mentioned the same thing to me. I am a little scared after hearing how they have treated the boys. I hope they both come home okay and soon.

I hope the next letter home will be from both Donald and me.

Always your loving daughter-in-law,
Rose

During the war, Rose probably wrote more letters than anyone except her mother-in-law. Donald endured the most combat of any of the Wilson brothers.

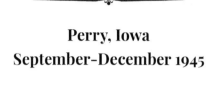

Perry, Iowa
September–December 1945

Clabe bought two Jersey cows. When the seller brought them to the acreage, Clabe sold the man a bushel of tomatoes.

And they bought a memorial stone for Junior's grave.

There was still no word on Dale or Danny.

The Wilsons spent their time working the farm, churning butter, and listening to news broadcasts hoping to hear that Dale had been liberated.

Sam and Darlene tried to come over every other Sunday to visit.

The Wilsons got to meet Evelyn and little Leora when Delbert and his new family arrived by train in Perry on September 21. Warren arrived in Des Moines soon after. It was a happy, but incomplete reunion.

That same week, Clabe signed for a carton from the Kansas City Quartermaster Depot. It held Danny's clothes, his watch, a small New Testament, and some souvenirs from his trip to the Army Air Force rest camp in Rome. There was a small bell charm stamped "Capri." Leora wore that charm for forty-two years, the rest of her life.

Each person who served in the armed forces was given a New Testament by the Gideons. In the front was an inscription by President Roosevelt, and an American flag on the opposite page. Danny had drawn an arrow pointing to the flag, and in his neat, bold handwriting added, "I give everything for the country it stands for."

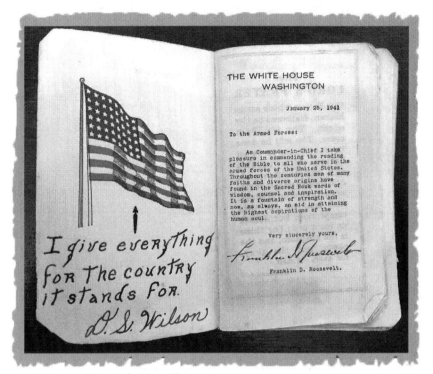

DANNY WILSON'S NEW TESTAMENT, RETURNED WITH THE REST
OF HIS EFFECTS, HAD A POIGNANT MESSAGE IN IT.

Donald docked in San Diego on a transport with 350 POWs, some in good shape, some not. "I'm still walking on air and trying to catch up on all the letters and back news," he wrote home. Don and Rose planned on taking a little time for themselves, a trip to see her folks, and then a trip back to Iowa. "I want to tell you all I can in person."

Donald and Rose eventually made it home for a nine-day visit. They did some hunting, stayed overnight with Sam and Darlene, stopped at the farm near Redfield which Warren and Doris were renting, visited friends and attended the annual Dexter-Earlham Thanksgiving football rivalry.

DON AND ROSE WILSON DROVE
THEIR STUDEBAKER BACK TO IOWA,
NOVEMBER 1945.

On November 21, Donna Gaye Wilson was born to Delbert and Evelyn.

That fall Clabe had done some work for Mr. Dorman, a neighboring farmer. He used some of the money to buy a couple of hound pups.

Leora bought a cedar chest, which would hold the precious family letters, telegrams, and papers that told her family's story of love and loss during WWII.

CHAPTER 18

Early 1946

Perry, Iowa
January 1946
Clabe and Leora

From the Adjutant General's Office in the War Department, Washington 25 D.C.

15 January 1946

Dear Mr. and Mrs. Wilson,

Since your son, Second Lieutenant Dale R. Wilson, Air Corps, was reported missing in action 27 November 1943, the War Department has entertained the hope that he survived and that information would be revealed dispelling the uncertainty surrounding his absence. However, as in many cases, the conditions of warfare deny us such information.

Public Law 490, 77th Congress, as amended, provided for a review and determination of the status of each person who has been missing in action for twelve months. Accordingly, your son's case was reviewed and he was continued in the status of missing in action as of November 1944. The law further provides that a subsequent review shall be made whenever warranted. Upon such subsequent review the making of a finding of death is authorized.

All available records and reports concerning the absence of your son have been carefully investigated and are deemed to warrant a subsequent review of his case. Information in the hands of the War Department indicates that your son was a crew member of a B-25 (Mitchell) bomber which participated in a strike mission to Wewak, New Guinea on 27 November 1943. The plane was hit by enemy anti-aircraft fire and was seen to crash in the water one and a half miles off the shore of Cape Boram, New Guinea.

After crashing into the water, the plane disintegrated, and the wreckage remained afloat but a short time before sinking. Observers from other planes failed to see any survivors emerge from the wreckage.

Since no information has been received which would support a presumption of his continued survival, the War Department must now terminate your son's absence by a presumptive finding of death. Accordingly, an official finding of death has been recorded. The finding does not establish an actual or probable date of death; however, as required by law, it includes a presumptive date of death for the purpose of termination of pay and allowances, settlement of accounts and payment of death gratuities. In the case of your son, this date has been set as 15 January 1946.

I regret the necessity for this message but trust that the ending of a long period of uncertainty may give at least some small measure of consolation. An appraisal of the sacrifice made by your son in the service of his country compels in us feelings of humility and respect. May Providence grant a measure of relief from the anguish and anxiety you have experienced during these many months.

Edward F. Witsell, Major General, Acting the Adjutant General of the Army

WASHINGTON DC, JAN. 22, 1946 CLABE D. WILSON, MINBURN, IOWA. THE SECRETARY OF WAR HAS ASKED ME TO EXPRESS HIS DEEP REGRET THAT YOUR SON 2ND LT DANIEL S WILSON WAS KILLED IN ACTION OVER AUSTRIA 19 FEBRUARY 1945. HE WAS PREVIOUSLY REPORTED MISSING IN ACTION. I REGRET THAT OFFICIAL REPORT RECEIVED ESTABLISHES HIS DEATH. CONFIRMING FOLLOWS E.F. WITSELL, ACTING ADJUTANT GENERAL

From the Adjutant General's Office in the War Department, Washington 25, D.C.

23 January 1946

Dear Mr. Wilson,

It is with deep regret that I am writing to confirm the recent telegram informing you of the death of your son, Second Lieutenant Daniel S. Wilson, Air Corps.

Your son was reported missing in action since 19 February 1945 over Austria. It has now been officially established from reports received in the War Department that he was killed in action on 19 February 1945 in an airplane crash in Schwanberg, Deutschlandsberg County, Austria.

I know the sorrow this message has brought you and it is my hope that in time the knowledge of his heroic sacrifice in the service of his country may be of sustaining comfort to you.

I extend to you my deepest sympathy.

Edward F. Witsell, Major General, Acting The Adjutant General of the Army

---

The Perry Daily Chief
February 6, 1946
Three Brothers Pay Supreme Sacrifice

Mr. and Mrs. Clabe Wilson, who live two miles southeast of Perry, are entitled to have a service flag in their window with five stars on it—three of them gold.

One of the hardest hit local families by the war, Mr. and Mrs. Wilson lost three sons during the recent world conflict. Another son was recently discharged from the navy and a fifth is still in the service.

Flight Officer Claiborne Junior Wilson, 20, youngest son of Mr. and Mrs. Wilson, was killed in a plane accident August 9 last year, at Aloe Field, Victoria, Texas.

Word has been received from the War Department that Lt. Dale R. Wilson, 24, who has been reported missing in action since Nov. 27, 1943, is now presumed dead. He was on a mission to New Guinea. [Dale was 22 when his plane was shot down.]

Dale received his wings at Roswell, New Mexico in Feb. 1943 and left for overseas in July of the same year. He served with the Fifth Air Force and was stationed at Port Moresby, New Guinea.

The War Department has notified the Wilsons that their son. Lt. Daniel S. Wilson, 22, who was previously reported as missing in action Feb. 19, 1945, is now reported killed in action on that date in a plane crash over Schwanberg, Austria. [Dan was 21.]

Daniel received his wings at Williams Field, Chandler, Arizona. He left for overseas in Oct. 1944 and was based with the 15th Air Force in Italy.

Two other sons of Mr. and Mrs. Wilson also served with the armed forces.

Delbert Wilson, 30, who had the rating of electrician's mate first class in the navy, is now home discharged after being in the service four years. Previous to his second enlistment he had served in the navy four years.

Chief Electrician Donald Wilson, 29, who has been in the navy 12 years, is now stationed in Seattle, Wash.

Perry, Iowa
May 1946
Leora & Clabe

Army Air Forces Headquarters sent the Wilsons what they had learned about Danny.

Dear Mr. and Mrs. Wilson,

In an effort to furnish the next of kin with all available details concerning casualties among our personnel, the Army Air Forces recently completed the translation of several volumes of captured German records.

In regard to Second Lieutenant Daniel S. Wilson, these records indicate that he was killed 19 February 1945, when his P-38 crashed at Schwanberg, four miles south of Deutsch-Landsberg, Austria. These records further state that his body was interred in the Cemetery of Schwanberg.

The Quartermaster General in his capacity as Chief, American Graves Registration Service is charged with the responsibility of notifying the next of kin concerning grave locations of members of the military forces who are killed or die outside of the continental limits of the United States. If the report of your son's burial has not been confirmed and you have not been notified by the Quartermaster General, that official will furnish definite information immediately upon receipt of the official report of interment from the Commanding General of Theater concerned.

May the knowledge of your son's valuable contribution to our cause sustain you in your bereavement.

Leon W. Johnson, Brigadier General, U.S.A., Chief Personnel Services Division

A family tradition was born on Decoration Day, 1946, which continued throughout the decades. The Wilson family gathered home-grown flowers to decorate the grave of a fallen son and brother.

Perry, Iowa
1946
Clabe

Leora pasted gold stars over three of the five blue ones on the service flag in their window. This new finality was heartbreaking.

Clabe had nightmares, vivid ones that haunted him. A lanky man anyway, many times when he sat down at a meal, he couldn't eat. He lost weight, and when he tried to rest, it only brought him memories and tears. It helped to have Delbert's little family close by, but Clabe was still depressed.

As if it all weren't too much anyway, both hunting dogs that he'd bought to keep him company were killed by the train not far from their home.

That autumn, Clabe, age 58, fell when he got out of bed. Delbert and Leora took him to Kings Daughters Hospital, where they learned he had a stroke. Leora stayed with him in the hospital until he was released.

It was hard for Clabe even after his release from the hospital. He had to concentrate on each swallow of eggnog.

In October, Doris brought her daughters, Joy (age 2) and Gloria Jean (4 months) to visit. Her father seemed to be improving.

But the next day Delbert called both sisters. Their dad had just died.

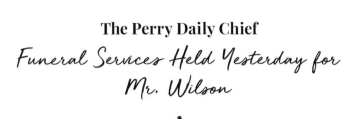

The Perry Daily Chief

Funeral Services Held Yesterday for Mr. Wilson

Funeral services for Claiborne (Clabe) D. Wilson, local farmer who died last Saturday, were held at 2:30 p.m. yesterday at the Workman Funeral Home.

The Rev. Lyle V. Newman of the First Christian Church officiated, and burial was in Violet Hill Cemetery.

Mr. Wilson, son of the late Mr. and Mrs. Daniel Wilson, was born Jan. 7, 1888 near Coon Rapids in Carroll County.

During his lifetime he farmed in various localities, including Guthrie Center, Dexter, and Minburn. He had moved to his present home about two years ago.

On Feb 15, 1914, he was married to Leora Goff, who survives. Also living are two sons, Delbert G. of Perry, and Donald W., who is in the navy; two daughters, Mrs. Warren D. Neal of Redfield and Mrs. Alvin C. Scar of Earlham; a half-brother, Fred Davis of Des Moines; three sisters, Mrs. Alice McLuen of Stuart, Mrs. Fonnie Kiggens of Boston, Mass., and Mrs. Verna Parrott of Des Moines, and several nieces and nephews.

Preceding him in death were three sons, all casualties of the recent war. They were Dale R., Daniel S., and Claiborne Junior.

1947

Official letters arrived asking if the Wilsons would like their son Daniel's remains to be sent back to Iowa. If they preferred, he would be buried near where he fell in an American cemetery in Europe. Leora decided the family could not go through another funeral. Since Dale had never been found and all three boys couldn't be laid to rest near each other, Leora signed the papers for Danny to be buried overseas.

When the permanent Lorraine American Cemetery was completed near St. Avold, France, Daniel Wilson's remains were reburied in Plot D, Row 5, Grave 7. A solemn ceremony was held, and an American flag was sent to his mother.

1948

After World War II and the loss of half of her family, Leora spent a winter in Omaha with her own widowed mother, Laura Goff. Laura had sons and grandchildren close by, but it was nice to have her oldest daughter staying with her.

LEORA (GOFF) WILSON AND HER MOTHER, LAURA (JORDAN) GOFF. TAKEN IN OMAHA BY LAURA'S GRANDSON MERRILL GOFF, WHO BECAME A COMMERCIAL PHOTOGRAPHER AFTER THE WAR. 1948

Leora was blessed with nine grandchildren, who all lived in Iowa. Those same old heart-tugs, the ones that always drove her to want to have a home of her own with her family close by, still nudged at her. Leora eventually brought her mother Laura back to Iowa, to a new little house in Guthrie Center.

Later, both surviving sons moved to the West Coast—Donald in Washington and Delbert in California.

LEORA WILSON

This wasn't the future Leora had anticipated even a handful of years ago, but she did have a snug home of her own where she was a companion for her mother for fourteen years until Laura's death in 1962. Both Darlene and Doris weren't far away, and made sure to visit often, to help her get groceries and run other errands, and take her for drives in the country to see where her history had taken place.

LEORA WILSON WITH SURVIVING CHILDREN AND SPOUSES, 1976.
LEFT: DONALD AND ROSE WILSON, SAM AND DARLENE SCAR,
WARREN AND DORIS NEAL, DELBERT AND EVELYN WILSON

And every year, Doris and Darlene took their mother to Perry's Violet Hill Cemetery to remember her husband and three sons who were lost during those terrible years.

Every spring, Danny Wilson's favorite yellow and black meadow-larks return to the Iowa landscape. Their welcome melodic ripple, sung from atop fenceposts, is at once hopeful and haunting.

1987
Obituary

Leora Frances Wilson, daughter of Laura Jordan and Milton S. Goff, was born in Guthrie County, Iowa, on December 4, 1890. She passed away at the Guthrie County Hospital, Guthrie Center, Iowa, on December 4, 1987.

Leora's early life was spent in the parental home attending school and growing into womanhood. On February 15, 1914, she was united in marriage to Claiborne Wilson. To this union ten children were born.

The family resided in Dexter, Minburn, and Perry and in 1948, [she] moved to Guthrie Center where Leora maintained her own home until her passing. She was a member of the VFW Auxiliary, the American Legion Auxiliary, Rebeccas, the Christian Women's Fellowship, and the First Christian Church of Guthrie Center.

Many became acquainted with Leora through the years by being a party of these various organizations, but also seeing her work in her yard and to make trips to town shopping. She took a good deal of pride in her flowers and enjoyed sharing them with church members on Sunday mornings.

Leora was preceded in death by her parents, her husband in 1946, six children, four brothers, and one sister.

To mourn her passing, she leaves her two sons, Delbert Wilson of Fremont, California, Donald Wilson of Raymond, Washington; two daughters, Mrs. Doris Neal and Mrs. Darlene Scar of Dexter,

Iowa. As well, there are 9 grandchildren, 18 great grandchildren, 1 great-great-grandchild, one sister, Mrs. Ruby Blockley of Long Beach, California, two brothers, Willis Goff of Redlin, Calif., and Clarence Goff of Omaha, Nebraska. As well, other relatives and friends will miss her.

EPILOGUE
2019
Joy Neal Kidney
Daughter of Doris Wilson Neal

No one in the family had ever been to see where Danny was buried. Aunt Darlene announced that she wanted to go. Delbert and Donald were both in their eighties at the time and didn't feel they could make the trip. My mother, Doris, was 79 but refused to ever fly after losing three brothers in the war.

It was decided I would accompany Aunt Darlene. As the keeper of the family history, having transcribed hundreds of letters and telegrams, and doing research through military records and WWII unit reunion groups, I'd appreciate the trip as much as anyone else. I had copies of Danny Wilson's 293 (casualty) file, which no one in the family had ever seen before my request. I even knew who buried this young pilot the first time—at the cemetery at Schwanberg, Austria. I had located a picture of my uncle Danny's wrecked plane in the town's history, and visiting his grave was something I had always wanted to do to honor him.

Once I told Mom I was going, and that my husband would also travel with us, she finally agreed to come along.

When we arrived at Lorraine American Cemetery at St. Avold, France, in October 1997, we placed a bouquet of gerbera daisies and roses on Danny's grave in Plot D, Row 5, just one among row after row of crosses and Stars of David—over 10,000 of them.

Surrounded by a lush chestnut grove, we stood under umbrellas while it drizzled. We held our own private ceremony for Mom and Aunt Darlene's younger brother, Danny Wilson, who lost his life at age 21 on February 19, 1945.

DORIS AND DARLENE AT THEIR
YOUNGER BROTHER'S GRAVE,
LORRAINE AMERICAN CEMETERY,
ST. AVOLD, FRANCE. OCTOBER 1997

The family is no longer able to take Memorial Day flowers to the Perry cemetery.

Junior has his own headstone. Dale and Danny's names and information are on another. Dale's date of death says 1946, which was the official finding of death. It gave no hint that he was a war casualty.

As I considered them, I realized that the headstones left too much unsaid. Could more information be added to old tombstones? We found out, yes. Just enough information was added to make it clear that this one rural, central Iowa family had endured the major loss of three sons during the war.

CENOTAPH, A MONUMENT FOR THOSE
BURIED ELSEWHERE, FOR DALE AND
DANNY WILSON, VIOLET HILL
CEMETERY, PERRY, IOWA.

HEADSTONE FOR
JUNIOR WILSON,
VIOLET HILL CEMETERY,
PERRY

On Clabe and Leora Wilson's stone is the list of all ten of their children. Even that new information stirs up stories the stones cannot tell: How all the children had whooping cough one awful winter during the Depression and the baby twins died of it. How baby Marilyn died of an enlarged heart while the older kids were at school.

About the two oldest brothers joining the navy after high school. Of Delbert's service during World War II, or that Donald had to tread water for an hour before being rescued from the sinking *Yorktown*, and the months of combat he'd been through.

That Leora, after she was widowed, made a home for her own mother for fourteen years. That her daughters carried on as farm wives, mothers with their own children in spite of the loss of three young brothers, then their father soon after.

And all the decades that the women in the family, year after year, remembered those young brothers on Memorial Day.

No, the tombstones cannot tell the whole story. And the people who lived during those World War II years are no longer alive.

Leora's fondest wish for her family to all be home and together did not happen this side of heaven.

But thanks to the letters and documents preserved as *Leora's Letters*—a collection of correspondence between the Wilson family during WWII, we will continue to remember the ultimate sacrifice these young brothers paid for the freedom we all enjoy today.

UPDATES ON
FAMILY MEMBERS

Clabe, Leora (who died in 1987, age 97), and Junior Wilson are buried in Violet Hill Cemetery, Perry, Iowa.

Delbert and Evelyn Wilson also had a son, Delbert Ross, born in Perry 1949. The family eventually moved to California where Delbert worked for the Lawrence Livermore National Laboratory. He died in 2000. His ashes were scattered at sea.

Donald Wilson lived in Washington State, doing commercial fishing. He retired from the Washington Department of Transportation and died in 1998. He and Rose had no children. They are buried at Naselle, Washington.

Doris (Wilson) Neal died in 2015, age 97. She and Warren are buried at Dexter, Iowa.

Darlene (Wilson) Scar died in 2019, age 97. She and Sam had two more sons—Dennis (born in 1949) and David (born in 1952). Sam and Darlene are buried at the Penn Center Cemetery in Madison County, near where they farmed.

Dale Wilson was never found. Only God knows where his remains lie. He is memorialized on the Tablets of the Missing, Manila American Cemetery, Manila, Philippines.

Danny Wilson is buried in Plot D, Row 5, in the Lorraine American Cemetery, St. Avold, France.

A memorial stone in Violet Hill Cemetery at Perry remembers both Dale and Danny.

USS *Yorktown*: The ship was discovered in 1998 by a team led by Robert Ballard, the undersea explorer who also found the wrecks of the *Titanic* and the German battleship *Bismarck*.

Dale's B-25: A film crew planned to use side-scanning sonar to try to locate their Mitchell bomber in 2005. Armed with copies of everything I could send them, they had planned to make a documentary about what they would find. But the diver who was leading the expedition had a massive heart attack as they got to Port Moresby. He was flown to Australia where he died. The attempt to find the plane was abandoned.

ACKNOWLEDGEMENTS

A big thank you to readers who offered feedback, even in the early days of the early "expanded" version. Readers and encouragers: Marilyn Bode, Jorja Dogic, Louise Hartman, Tom Honz, and Gloria Neal.

Also several writers:

* Elaine Briggs, author of *Joe Dew, a Glorious Life*, her father's story. Elaine has been such an encourager throughout these final months.

* Anne Clare, author of the WWII historical novel *Whom Shall I Fear?*

* Mike Flinn, author of several books, including historical novels.

* Mary Potter Kenyon, author of several nonfiction books, including *Expressive Writing for Healing.*

* Richard L. Muniz, writing as William R. Ablan, author of *The Lawman: Against Flesh and Blood*, the first in a trilogy of police stories.

* Patti Stockdale, author of *Three Little Things*, due out in 2020, a World War I historical novel based on letters of her grandparents.

* Olivia Vander Ploeg, fantasy writer.

Professional help:

* Robin Grunder, ghostwriter and founder of Legacy Press.

* Anne Stratton Philo Fleck.

* Renee Fisher, owner, and operator of Renee Fisher & Co.

Other encouragers:

* Historian and Dexter Museum Board member Rod Stanley,
  along with the rest of the Dexter Museum Board—Doris Feller,
  Gloria Neal, Patricia Hochstetler. Also Dexter Librarian
  Mary McColloch.

* Jeanette Peel-Peddicord and the Perry Preservation Society.

* The Dallas County Freedom Rock Committee:
  Larry Cornelison, Cari Wooten-Fuller, Margie Kenyon,
  Deanette Snyder, Carolyn Snyder, Mark Golightly.

* Nicholas Dowd, poet, who grew up in Guthrie Center, Iowa.

* Guy Kidney, steadfast chauffeur.

WHERE TO LEARN MORE
ABOUT THE WILSON FAMILY

Dexter Museum, Dexter, Iowa - large display. (The family lived there during the Great Depression. Five Wilson children graduated from Dexter High School.)

Dallas County Freedom Rock, Minburn, Iowa (Where the family lived during WWII until all five sons were in the service. Two graduated from the nearby Washington Township School.)

THE FIVE WILSON BROTHERS ARE HONORED ON THE
DALLAS COUNTY FREEDOM ROCK AT MINBURN, IOWA,
WHICH WAS DEDICATED IN OCTOBER 2019.

Ray Michael Sorensen II is founder and artist of **The Freedom Rock**. thefreedomrock.com

Perry, Iowa: Forest Park Museum - poster. (Clabe and Leora bought an acreage south of Perry after all their sons had left for the service.)

Also **Violet Hill Cemetery**

🌐 **joynealkidney.com** (especially under the Depression Era and WW II categories)

🅵 **https://www.facebook.com/joy.kidney**

And Joy Neal Kidney writer at:

📷 https://www.instagram.com/joynealkidney/

✉️ joynealkidney@gmail.com

Would you please leave a review of the book on Goodreads and/or Amazon?

DISCUSSION QUESTIONS

1. Do you have family members who served in World War II, or at another time in our history? Has anyone recorded their stories? How could you make sure they are?

2. Memorial Day is dedicated to remember Americans lost in wars. If your family has no combat losses, how do you make sure to remember them on Memorial Day? How could you help the next generations think about the nation's great losses?

3. Thousands of graves of young American lie in foreign countries which our soldiers helped free from tyranny. They have regular ceremonies to remember and reflect. Because WW II was fought on foreign soil, does that affect your perspective about American losses?

4. What do you think motivated the Wilson brothers to enlist? What motivates people today to join the military?

5. Several family members advised the youngest brother to stay home with their parents. How might that have eventually changed family dynamics from his point of view? What about his parents?

6. What did the Wilson family do to cope with all the uncertainty during the war? For months after the war, the Wilsons still had no answers about what had happened to two of their sons. How did they get through those anxious days? What would you have done?

7. Essie Sharpton was a faithful correspondent for Leora through the decades, helping to sustain and encourage her. Has someone in your life come alongside when things have been tough? Have you been able to do the same for someone else?

8. C.S. Lewis said, "I have seen great beauty of spirit in come who were great sufferers." (*The Problem of Pain*) Have you known someone with a sweet spirit in spite of physical or emotional pain? What do you think sustains them?

9. There's something precious about being able to hold and keep a letter, a tangible blessing. People during World War II sometimes had to wait weeks for one, heightening the tension families already felt. Do you have any old family letters? Why do you think people keep them for decades?

CLASSROOM TOPICS OF DISCUSSION AND ACTIVITIES

With thanks to Elaine Briggs

1. Have students chose a brother and complete maps of their various locations stationed during the war.

2. Have students choose a brother and complete a timeline for him, including what training he received and where he was sent for combat.

3. How do the letters let you know farming was very important to the war effort?

4. What was the attitude of the brothers for serving in the war? Give examples.

5. Explain how important letters were to both those who served and those at home.

6. Why do you think censoring of the mail was important?

7. Food was rationed during WW II. Why do you suppose the Wilsons didn't mention it much?

8. How was life during WW II complicated by having no electricity?

Made in the USA
Monee, IL
29 June 2022

98747379R00203